D1524126

The
SPLENDOR
of His Ways

And now men cannot look on the light when it is
bright in the skies,
When the wind hath passed, and cleared them.
Out of the north cometh golden splendor:
God hath upon him terrible majesty.
—JOB 37.21–22

Ye have heard of the endurance of Job, and have seen the end of the Lord, how that the Lord is full of pity, and merciful.

—JAMES 5.11

The
Splendor
of His Ways

SEEING THE LORD'S END IN JOB

STEPHEN KAUNG

Christian Fellowship Publishers, Inc.
New York

Available from the Publishers at:

11515 Allecingie Parkway
Richmond, VA 23235-4301

Foreword

COUNTLESS VOLUMES have been written about the story of Job. And almost without exception all of them have devoted considerable space to what is most often singled out as being its central theme—the problem of suffering and Job's endurance of it. Understandably, a suffering humanity is easily drawn to the drama of this venerable man's heroic struggle against every manner of trouble and deprivation which came his way.

Yet without minimizing the important place suffering occupies in this Old Testament narrative nor ignoring the helpful lesson to be derived from a study of Job's endurance, the author of *The Splendor of His Ways* sees the primary thought of the story as lying elsewhere. Stephen Kaung feels we must look beneath the phenomenon of Job's sufferings if we would apprehend the story's real lesson. For he sees Job's experience of manifold trials as being but the surface of things: it is not the main concern of the narrative. Even though the suffering process is admittedly an essential element in JOB it serves only to tell us what is going on; it does not tell us to what end or purpose it points.

Just here a fragment from the New Testament proved to be quite helpful to the author and became for him the key to the entire book. "Ye have seen the end of the Lord, " wrote the apostle James, "how that the Lord is full of pity, and merciful." End here means purpose; it also signifies the very last, the final thing; which is therefore to say, that God's purpose—the finality of the Lord—was eventually realized in the life of God's suffering servant. For at his "latter end" (as his Bible narrator significantly terms it) Job received from the Lord twice as much as he had had before, an event not unlike the double portion of a father's substance which any Hebrew firstborn son would later in life be entitled to receive as his birthright.

What then is the chief lesson of JOB? Briefly stated, it is sonship. It is the full maturing into *sons* of the children of God through whatever ways God deems best to achieve His purpose of their being conformed to the image of His beloved Son, who himself becomes the Firstborn among many brethren (Rom. 8.29). And though the ways He selects may sometimes seem dark and cruel, as Job himself once thought, they in reality are full of splendor and benevolence; because at the end God is proven to have been full of compassion and pity throughout. Although perhaps hard to believe, even in His drastic stripping of Job the Lord still emerges as a God of love and mercy, as is shown by His bringing this man to His marvelous end.

Yet what is by far the most remarkable feature about this new study of JOB is the manner in which the author treats the important middle section of the narrative (Chs. 3–37), prompted as this treatment is by the symbolism he perceptively ascribes to Job's three friends and to the young man Elihu. Mr. Kaung agrees completely with the generally accepted view that the words of Eliphaz, Bildad, and Zophar, in their attempts at solving Job's spiritual dilemma, are representative of the kinds of answers which mysticism, traditionalism, and dogmatism would characteristically bring to the problem. He considers these, however, to be but *outward* representations. For him the three friends can also have meaning in an *inward* way. In this respect they symbolize the deep searchings of a person's soul in the three areas of the emotion, mind, and will as a man goes through the furnace of an inexplicable personal trial. The voice of Job and the voices of these friends are the voices of a man's inner depths as he struggles within himself to penetrate the darkness that has enveloped him and so find his way through to God.

On the other hand Elihu, whose words have so often been dismissed by scholars as being simply a later interpolation or at best merely an afterthought added by the original author, is seen by Mr. Kaung as standing uniquely for the human spirit—that innermost part of man for perceiving the divine Spirit. Like young Elihu to Job, the newly regenerated spirit, once the agitated soul has been quieted, will be able to interpret to the believer the mind and will of the Lord and thus pave the way for the real solution to the problem: the appearing of God himself.

Now it is this unusual treatment of Job that has lent a high degree of originality to the present study. The book therefore makes a significant contribution to our understanding of a difficult and often mystifying portion of the Scriptures. Indeed, some re-interpretation of this

Old Testament story may quite possibly occur as a result.

Yet the burden of the author was hardly concerned with such matters as these when he first presented the substance of this volume in a special sequence of spoken ministry. For anyone reading Mr. Kaung's words today will recognize how far removed from such intellectual pursuits that burden was, and still is. For pervading the entire work is the author's earnest desire to help his audience to see and experience afresh the glorious design the Father has for His children, to help his readers to understand anew that the ways He chooses to effect it in them are most kind and compassionate, and to encourage them to seek the kind of heart attitude toward God and His rule which must ever be one of reverential fear and humility.

May that burden, now doubly discharged, become the burden of all who read these pages. May all be willing to learn the lesson of sonship. And then the triumphant story of Job can be their story too.

—The Editor

New York
April 1974

Preface

THE BOOK of Job is a very rich and precious portion of the Old Testament writings. And in any treatment of it, the book can be approached from many different directions and can yield innumerable lessons to benefit one's spiritual life. Any exhaustive study of Job is therefore completely out of the question for the all too brief treatment of it now in the reader's hands. The intention has been instead to focus attention primarily upon what to me has seemed, after many months of meditation before the Lord, to be the central lesson which the Spirit of God may be desiring to teach us all.

In view of this limited scope and purpose, I have therefore concentrated upon one particular approach to the book of Job. A rough sketch of it is to be found in the next paragraph, where I indicate a simple outline of the Scripture narrative for the reader. Yet I wish to make clear that this is not the only nor even perhaps the best approach; it is but one among many ways a person may consider this sacred book and so obtain by the Lord's grace some spiritual profit from its pages to the glory of God.

Now as aids to our consideration of Job together, I would like to make two suggestions. First of all, let us divide this rather lengthy Old Testament poem into four major segments, which can be conveniently marked out as follows:

Chapters 1–2, The Crisis
Chapters 3–31, The Searching of the Soul
Chapters 32–37, The Spirit's Interpretation
Chapters 38–42, God's Appearing

By this outline division the reader can perhaps discern the approach to the book I have chosen to take; namely, that a crisis comes into the life of Job precipitating the entire Scripture story: and in keeping with this approach, we shall follow this man in his crisis of both soul and spirit until it is finally terminated and only resolved when God appears to him. That in brief is the plan we shall adopt in our treatment together of this precious Old Testament narrative. And the reader will note that the four divisions of the narrative marked out above correspond exactly to the four Parts of the study to follow. So that if this very simple outline can be kept in mind throughout these pages it may assist in giving some sense of direction.

But secondly, I would hope the reader would take the time to actually read the book of Job as our treatment of it unfolds. Otherwise, I am afraid it may be somewhat difficult to follow clearly what is said here. For we cannot stay to consider the wealth of detail to be found in JOB. Perhaps one method could be to read *beforehand* each section of the Biblical account corresponding to the particular Part covered in the study. Yet whichever way he chooses to use, the reader, I believe, can benefit so much more from what is to follow if he looks thoroughly into the Scripture account itself in conjunction with what is written here.

May the Holy Spirit, on whom alone we must rely, open up to God's children this rich treasure from the sacred writings. May the pages of this limited volume which now goes out be used by the Lord to help us all to trust Him more deeply—regardless our circumstances—so as to arrive at His desired end of becoming matured sons of God.

Editor's Note

A word should be appended regarding the sources for the material found in the following pages. First, the substance of the four Parts making up this volume was originally a sequence of messages which the author delivered in New York at a special church conference held during the New Year's weekend, January 1971. And second, as an added enrichment to the entire volume, the author kindly loaned to the editor his set of private preparatory notes containing many gold nuggets scattered throughout, a sizeable number of which never found their way into the messages subsequently spoken but are now included here.

Scripture quotations are from the
American Standard Version
of the Bible (1901),
unless otherwise indicated.

PART ONE

The Crisis

Behold, he is in thy hand;
    Only spare his life.
        —THE LORD GOD TO SATAN

I feared a fear, and it hath come upon me,
    And that which I dreaded hath come to me.
I was not in safety, neither had I quietness,
    neither was I at rest,
    And trouble came.
        —JOB THE SERVANT OF GOD

The Crisis

THE BOOK of Job is considered to be the oldest book in the entire Bible. It may very well be the first written Hebrew sacred record; for chronologically, it may be dated before the five books of Moses. Most likely the man Job lived during the period of the Hebrew patriarchs and so was probably a contemporary of Abraham or Isaac or even Jacob.

Now Job is not a fictitious name. The Bible character known to us under this name is a real person. The reason this can be asserted is the fact that not only do we have this book of Job but also we find that the name of Job is mentioned in several other places in the Scriptures. Ezekiel 14.14 reads as follows: "Though these three men Noah, Daniel, and Job, were in [the land], they should deliver but their own souls by their righteousness, saith the Lord Jehovah." Moreover, this same refrain is repeated in verse 20: "Though Noah, Daniel, and Job, were in it, as I live, saith the Lord Jehovah, they should deliver neither son nor daughter; they should but deliver their own souls by their righteousness." Hence in the book of the prophet Ezekiel Job is listed together with Noah and Daniel. In addition, Job's righteousness is noted. He is a righteous man who is classed with both Noah and Daniel. And since those two men were real people, we can doubtless conclude that Job too was a real person.

The name of Job is mentioned in the New Testament as well—in the Epistle of James: "Behold, we call them blessed that endured: ye have heard of the endurance of Job" (5.11 mg.). Even the apostle James referred to his name. So that at least these two places in both Testaments do in fact show us that this man Job is a real individual. He is not a fictitious character.

It should also be pointed out that there are two places in the New Testament where a passage in the book of Job is quoted. 1 Corinthians 3.19 quotes almost verbatim from Job 5.13, and in Matthew 24.28 the Lord Jesus refers specifically back to the words found in Job 39.30. We see, then, that not only the *name* of Job is mentioned—in both the Old Testament and the New—but furthermore, the *book* of Job is quoted in the New Testament. Hence here are proofs that this narrative belongs to the sacred record and that Job is a real person.

This man Job (who most likely lived, as has been said, during the time of the patriarchs) dwelt in the land of Uz. This area was presumably the land of Edom. Yet we do not know whether Job was a son of Edom or whether, being a son of Jacob, he had perhaps moved to Uz and had thus lived to the south of the Promised Land, it being a desert place. In any event, Job made his home in this place and became very prosperous and achieved a high station in life. For he was a man who could easily be considered a sheik, a desert prince—perhaps even a king—among his own people (cf. 29.25). But of even greater significance, Job was a chosen one of God.

Is it not strange, however, that the first recorded history within the sacred writings refers to a man outside the pale of Israel? Will we not naturally think that the first recorded history in the Hebrew canon should surely refer to Israel or to a son of Israel? Quite surprisingly, though, we discover that the first sacred record speaks of a man outside of Israel, before the Jewish nation is formed and is separated from the rest of the world.

Is there a reason for this? Conceivably, through this earliest book God is trying to tell us that so far as His original purpose is concerned He is dealing with mankind as a whole. True, God does choose the nation of Israel; but His choosing of the Jewish nation is a matter of His plan—of His economy and administration—rather than a matter of His purpose. So far as God's purpose is concerned, we know that there is no partiality with Him. His purpose is above and beyond all limits of nationality, race, class, and so forth. He is not as exclusive as some people would like to make Him. Quite the reverse, we find that God has the totality of mankind before Him; and that this is probably the reason why, instead of it being the record of a son of Israel which is first set down in the Scriptures, it turns out to be the history of Job—a man who most likely does not belong to Israel at all.

Moreover, according to one line of tradition, some believe that it was Moses himself who introduced the book of Job into the sacred literature of the Jewish nation, that it was Moses who translated it and placed it into what we now know as the Old Testament canon. Whether or not this is the fact we are not sure, but will it not be even more wonderful and more amazing if this should be the case? And why? Because the Hebrew lawgiver is not as exclusive as later on some of the Jewish people themselves became. On the contrary, Moses was willing to introduce the story of this man Job, a non-Jew, into the Jewish canonical writings. He was open to all the works of God. May we therefore approach this book of Job with just such an open and enlarged heart too. Whenever there is a soul who seeks after God, and no matter who he may be, he is accepted and approved of Him. God will reveal himself to that one, even as in the New Testament period He did so to Cornelius the gentile Roman centurion (cf. Acts 10, esp. vv.34,35).

Hence as we come to this first written portion of the Bible—referring as it does to a man who lived long before the formation of the Jewish nation—we must recognize that God has the entire human race in view; and because of this divine fact we shall come to perceive that this book does not deal primarily with God's plan but basically with His purpose. And this is an important distinction which must not be lost sight of in our treatment of JOB.

BUT JUST WHO was this man Job? What kind of person was he? Chapter 1, verse 1 tells us this: "There was a man in the land of Uz, whose name was Job; and that man was perfect and upright, and one that feared God, and turned away from evil." Simply put, Job was a perfect and upright man, one who feared God and turned away or abstained from evil. Such is the biblical writer's description of that man. And this description is recognized and accepted even by God himself, because when He subsequently challenged Satan He gave the very same estimate of this man: "Hast thou considered my servant Job? for there is none like him in the earth, a perfect and an upright man, one that feareth God, and turneth away from evil" (1.8). We need to see that this is not only some description set down by man but this characterization is recognized even by God (and, incidentally, it was even noticed and acknowledged by Satan as well).

Before us, then, is the book of Job which opens up with a man who is not a beginner. Job is not at all a novice. He is a man who, as we commence to read his story, has already attained to a high position before God. He already had moved well ahead of all the people in the world in respect of both piety and righteousness. We are dealing here, not with one who is a beginner in the Lord, but with one who has arrived at a certain level of spiritual life already, and the story before us commences at that level. This fact needs to be kept in mind constantly by anyone who would more accurately study this Old Testament narrative.

Let us look more closely at the description of this man. *First of all,* Job was described as being perfect and upright. This word perfect does not mean sinless perfection. "Perfect" or "complete" in the Bible always means "matured". Use of the word perfect does not signify that Job has attained a position or state where he cannot sin and where he does not and will not sin. No, not that at all; for none is sinless perfect except the incarnated Son of God. Perfect here refers to his heart. So far as Job's heart condition toward God is concerned he is in this regard a matured person. Desiring nothing but God himself, he in his being is all out toward Him. So far as his knowledge goes, to that extent he tries to be obedient to God. He did all that he knew. He may consequently be considered blameless before God, because his heart is perfect toward the Lord. And nothing pleases the Lord more than a perfect heart.

In the Old Testament this is a very very precious thing. It is said of David that he served God with a perfect heart (see 1 Kings 9.4, 11.4, 14.8, 15.3,5). Yet it does not mean that David never fails—that David never sins; nevertheless, we find that he pleased the Lord. And how? Because he had a perfect heart toward Him. With some of the other Jewish kings, they undeniably did what was right in the sight of God and yet they did not serve Him with a heart like David's. We may do everything exactly right but our inner condition may not be perfect toward God. A perfect heart is far more precious than doing everything correct in His sight. Perfection refers more to the inner attitude, whereas righteousness is a term which has reference more to acts and deeds. Some people may do things right but their heart is not blameless before the Lord, and the Lord is one who looks into our heart. And what He loves is a perfect heart.

Recall what is said in 2 Chronicles 16.9: "The eyes

of Jehovah run to and fro throughout the whole earth, to show himself strong in the behalf of them whose heart is perfect toward him." The eyes of the Lord run back and forth through the whole earth looking for something. Looking for what? He is looking for anyone with a perfect heart, and whenever He finds that kind of condition He will show himself strong on that one's behalf. He will stand by him. And this is the kind of heart He wants in all of us.

Do we today serve God with such a heart or do we often find ourselves in the condition of a double heart, which literally signifies, a heart *and* a heart? Yes, we do love God, we do have a heart for Him, but at the same time we have another heart for the world as well: a heart and a heart.

Job, though, was one who desired nothing but God himself—and this, in spite of all his weaknesses. Yes indeed, he might have weakness; even so, his heart was centered upon God: he desired the Lord above everything else: he wanted Him and Him alone. And that was the condition of this man Job: He was perfect in heart toward God.

Yet the record also declares that he was upright too. As a matter of fact, a perfect heart always goes together with righteousness. Because his heart was perfect before the Lord, therefore his deeds and actions before men were righteous and upright. He did everything right in the sight of both God and man. The righteousness of Job, we know, is proverbial. As we saw earlier, he in this respect is classed by God with both Noah and Daniel (Ez. 14.14,20). We are well-acquainted with the patience of Job, but we tend to forget that the righteousness of Job must come before Job's patience. Because he is righteous, therefore he is patient.

But secondly in the description given of God's servant, this perfectness and this uprightness of Job are further set forth by the use of these two phrases: feareth the Lord, and, turneth away or abstaineth from evil. Actually, these *explain* his perfection and righteousness. We must understand that in Old Testament times the heart that is perfect toward the Lord is one which in the first place fears the Lord: "The fear of the Lord is the beginning of wisdom"—and this is the teaching of the entire Old Testament thought. Anyone's reading of Proverbs will yield the same conclusion as the author Solomon himself came to, namely, that the fear of the Lord is the beginning of wisdom (9.10). And coming to the book of Job we learn that it too expresses this thought (see for instance, 28.28). In fact, the entire Old Testament can be summed up in these very words: the fear of the Lord. In that period of God's people the fear of the Lord was alone judged to be the highest and best which a person could ever reach. To God's people of that day it alone constituted the greatest wisdom to be found. In short, the fear of the Lord was for that age the summit of spiritual life. And whoever feared the Lord had his heart perfect before Him.

When we come to the New Testament period, however, we learn that we need something more than simply the fear of the Lord. A turning to 2 Corinthians Chapter 5 will show that there are *two* things in view, not just one: Yes, there is a knowing the fear of the Lord on the one hand, but there is also a being constrained by the love of Christ as well (see vv.11 and 14). Since

22

the inception of the New Testament era the fear of God is not considered enough; there must in addition be a love of Christ. The love of Christ constrains me; and *that* constitutes the New Covenant concept of perfectness. Unquestionably, we must fear God. I am afraid Christians today are somewhat too bold at times. Frequently there is a lack of reverence toward God. We become too loose. We do not fear Him as we ought. It is important that we fear the Lord. Nevertheless, there must be something more. We must be constrained by the love of Christ. This we see clearly in the New Testament.

And finally, we have in the description of Job this phrase, abstaining from evil. To us today this characterization seems so very negative, yet it is the first step toward righteousness. We must see that righteousness in the Old Testament sense *is* an abstaining from evil. Righteousness in those ancient times was much more negative in approach than positive. For instance, take note of the Ten Commandments. What do you find there? Strictly speaking, you find that only one commandment is positive while the rest are negative. Is this not true? "Thou shalt not" is much more prominent than "Thou shalt". Thou shalt have no other gods. Negative. Thou shalt not make any image. Negative. Thou shalt not call upon the name of the Lord in vain. Negative. Thou shalt not do anything on the Sabbath day. Negative. Thou shalt not, thou shalt not, thou shalt not. It is almost totally negative. Only the commandment to honor one's father and mother is positive. Hence due to the fact that in the Old Testament time the work of redemption has as yet not been revealed, the very meaning of righteousness during that ancient period was almost exclusively couched in negative terms. So that an "abstaining from evil" was considered righteous.

Nevertheless, as in the case just mentioned above of fearing the Lord, when we come to the New Testament writings we discover that negative righteousness is simply not enough. For the fuller meaning of righteousness can only come to us through our Lord Jesus Christ. And Jesus in the Gospel of John unfolds to us this fuller meaning in those words of His recorded in Chapter 16: "I go away . . . [and] I will send [the Holy Spirit] unto you. And he, when he is come, will convict the world in respect of . . . righteousness, *because I go to the Father,* and ye behold me no more" (vv.7,8,10). Here is the *full* meaning of righteousness. Righteousness is not only, negatively, an abstaining from evil; it is even more so, in positive terms, an entering into the very presence of God. In other words, not only should we not sin but also we should be able to stand before God. That is the full meaning of righteousness in the New Testament sense. Who can enter and stand before the very presence of God and live there? Only the one who is righteous, and that is precisely where our Lord Jesus is. Christ himself is our righteousness, and we approach God and live before Him *only* in Christ. And that is true righteousness. But let us remember that in the Old Covenant period the righteousness principally in view and at which a person can arrive is the abstaining from evil.

Before us, then, is this man Job, a person who was perfect and upright in heart, one who feared God, and who abstained from evil. We must be careful not to judge him by our New Testament standard; rather

24

should we recognize that in a certain respect we have before us a specimen, the *best* specimen if you please, of godly life and piety which we can envisage in that Old Testament day. This in reality is what God himself declares to Satan concerning His servant (see 1.8). There is at his time no one on earth who is more perfect than Job. There is at his time no one on earth who is more righteous than Job. There is no one on earth who fears the Lord more than Job. And there is no one on earth who abstains from evil more than Job. In short, we have in this man the finest example of the Old Testament perfection. And God was pleased with him and God was proud of him. So much so, that He was even able to challenge Satan with him. Such was His confidence in Job that God had no hesitation in challenging His arch enemy with this man and, further, in allowing Satan to tempt him to the uttermost. In this regard, I sometimes wonder just how much *we* have pleased God and to what extent He can trust us and boast of us—we who have more privileges than Job, we who by the circumstance of a later epoch ought to be even something more. I wonder.

Now THIS MAN Job lived peacefully and prosperously. He had a wonderful family, with seven sons and three daughters; and all of them were good. Although he had raised such a big family, all his children were nonetheless dutiful and obedient. For this man—and his wife who went along with him—had brought them up in the fear of the Lord and in the abstinence from evil.

Later, Job's family was greatly enlarged when each of the seven sons began to have his own family and his own house. And we know that all of them enjoyed life, because there was frequent feasting and merry-making —yet without them sinning against God because their father kept them in a right condition before the Lord.

Then too, there was perfect harmony between the parents and the children. We know that, though grown up, they were still obedient to their parents in certain important respects. For example, when, after their days of feasting among themselves, Job would arise and say, "Now that the day of feasting is over, we must offer sacrifice lest in the time of feasting my children curse God"—these children of his were very willing to follow his counsel and have a sacrifice offered to God. They were most obedient, not like so many young people of this current age.

Yet besides the harmony which existed between parents and children, we can also observe that these sons and daughters of Job—even though they were adults—maintained such a love and harmony *among themselves*. Often, when children grow up they tend each to go his or her own way. But here was a family that was truly united. Feastings occurred one after another; but when each of the sons was having his own party he would have every one of his other brothers and sisters over as well. What harmony existed among them all!

But of course, in witnessing such a thing we recognize that there must be a background to it. It did not just happen. It must have come about through the admonition and wise discipline of the Lord given to these children by their parents. Hence we can say that Job had not only attained to a very high degree of righteousness before the Lord himself but in addition had led his entire household with him to the feet of God. How blessed this must have been. Especially in view of family life today, this is something much to be admired. And God in turn blessed and prospered Job. God gave him many properties and enabled him to have numerous servants. He became very great, greater than all the people in the East (1.3b); so much so that he was considered a prince of the desert, a king among his own people.

YET IF YOU want to know what kind of a life Job actually lived during the period covered by these initial verses of the Bible narrative—that is, the period before the coming of his trials—you can detect only a very small amount by reading those few early verses. There he is described as having been perfect, upright, one who feared God and abstained from evil. His family is pictured as having been in harmony, in unity, in love. And his possessions are shown as having been in great abundance. But if you want to know more fully how he really lived before the Lord you have to turn to Chapter 29. For it was in that chapter that Job tried to recall those former days when he was under the favor of God. Hear him as he spoke to his three friends:

Oh that I were as in the months of old,
  As in the days when God watched over me;
When his lamp shined above my head,
  And by his light I walked through darkness;
As I was in the ripeness of my days,
  When the counsel of God was upon my tent;
When the Almighty was yet with me,
  And my children were about me;
When my steps were washed with butter,
  And the rock poured me out streams of oil!

When I went forth to the gate unto the city,
  When I prepared my seat in the broad place,
The young men saw me and hid themselves,
  And the aged rose up and stood;
The princes refrained from talking,
  And laid their hand on their mouth;
The voice of the nobles was hushed,
  And their tongue cleaved to the roof
  of their mouth.
For when the ear heard me, then it blessed me;
  And when the eye saw me, it gave witness
  unto me:
Because I delivered the poor that cried,
  The fatherless also, and him that had none
  to help him.
The blessing of him that was ready to perish came
  upon me;
  And I caused the widow's heart to sing for joy.
I put on righteousness, and it clothed me:
  My justice was as a robe and a turban.
I was eyes to the blind,

And feet was I to the lame.
I was a father to the needy:
And the cause which I knew not I searched out.
And I brake the jaws of the unrighteous,
And plucked the prey out of his teeth.

Then I said, I shall die in my nest,
And I shall multiply my days as the sand:
My root is spread out to the waters,
And the dew lieth all night upon my branch:
My glory is fresh in me,
And my bow is renewed in my hand.

Unto me men gave ear, and waited,
And kept silence for my counsel.
After my words they spake not again;
And my speech distilled upon them.
And they waited for me as for the rain;
And they opened their mouth wide as for the
latter rain.
I smiled on them, when they had no confidence;
And the light of my countenance they cast not
down.
I chose out their way, and sat as chief,
And dwelt as a king in the army,
As one that comforteth the mourners. (vv.2–25 mg.)

Job began by saying, "Oh that I were as in the months of old, as in the days when God watched over [or preserved] me" (vv.1–2). By this time he had been in the crucible of trial for several months. Some have even suggested that at this point it might have been as long as a year. We can at least say that quite a few months have

29

passed. And as he was experiencing that trial of his for so many months he recalled in great detail the days when God had preserved him. He knew and acknowledged that before this trial had come it had been the Lord who in those days had preserved him. And notice how he described his days: they were days "when his lamp shined upon my head, and by his light I walked through darkness" (v.3). The light of God shone over and around him. The light of Jehovah led his way. Job, in other words, was not only protected by God, he was guided by Him too. There was no lacking in light. God illuminated him even when all was darkness, so that he walked in light: he was not groping amidst clouds and mist. He knew God and God gave him light so that he could walk through every dark circumstance.

Job continued. "I was in the ripeness of my days, when the counsel of God was upon my tent; when the Almighty was yet with me" (vv.4,5a). In the Hebrew language the phrase "the ripeness of my days" literally means "my days of autumn"—"I was in the days of my autumn . . ." In other words, Job viewed himself, before the great testing had come upon him, as having arrived at spiritual maturity already. In essence he was saying: In the days of my autumn, in the days of my maturity, when the counsel of God was over my tent, God spoke to me. I communed with the Lord and He told me His secret. God was still with me.

Job, therefore, was a man full of spiritual illumination, a man who was given great wisdom by the Lord. He was a person who understood the mysteries of God, the secret counsel of God. The Lord was with him. He was indeed with him: his steps were bathed in milk and butter, and the rock poured out beside him rivers of oil. In a word, we find that all Job's steps were covered with the abundance of God. And as we read further on through Chapter 29 we discover he has attained to such a degree of spirituality (if we may so call it) that whenever he came out among his people the young men would slip away, the old ones would stand up, the princes would refrain from speaking, and the nobles would hush their voices. Whenever *he* spoke, everybody listened. Moreover, Job was eyes to the blind, feet to the lame, father to the needy, and a judge to all. His way was altogether noble and righteous.

Read this entire chapter and then you *really* see what a life Job lived. How beautiful and perfect in heart he walked before God, and how pure and righteous was his conversation and behavior in the world. How blameless he was. Job could honestly say before the Lord, as we notice in Chapter 31, that so far as he knew he had done everything which was right. We therefore observe here one who had the light of the Spirit of God. One who had the presence of God. One who was under the guidance and the illumination of God. One who was watched over, protected, and preserved by God. One whose ways were full of the abundance of God. And one who was great among his people and who performed countless commendable deeds:

Now AS WE listen to Job tell it I am afraid we will all

agree that he had truly arrived. For certainly *he* thought he had. He judged that he had arrived at the very end, that he had climbed to the summit, to the very peak of life. Yet please notice that this is only where the story of Job actually begins. And that is the very reason why this book is somewhat difficult; because unless the reader can see where it commences he will not be able to appreciate all which is recorded in the book thereafter.

May I say again that the narrative of Job is not the record of a beginner in God, but the story of one who knew the Lord, one who had gone some distance with God. Yet if it is not the account of a beginner, neither is it one of maturity. It is somewhere in between. On the one hand you do find a man who feared the Lord and abstained from evil, who knew God to a very large extent and was under His protection, guidance and blessing. You in fact find a man who had rich fellowship with the Lord and out of this fellowship he was able to teach, to instruct, and to help so many. On the other hand you will come to perceive that there was much that God had yet to do with his life in order to bring him to the desired end. And the whole narrative in JOB refers to just that necessary work of God. Do you follow me? The story does not open with the *inauguration* of a spiritual life. It commences with a man's life that has gone on with the Lord for some time and has attained to a certain point where he even assumes he *has* arrived. His spiritual condition is such that Job regards himself as having reached maturity. He believes he is in the days of his autumn. He concludes that there can be nothing more to be achieved. And that he could live on peacefully and prosperously in his nest forever (see

29.18–19). But he is terribly deceived. He in fact is the victim of his own illusion.

❦

HOWEVER, IT IS precisely at this juncture that God begins to work in that life in order to bring him to the real end—full maturity. For this he clearly lacked. Yes, Job had attained somewhat and had gotten somewhere, but hidden deep within him was a secret fear. And this fear he finally though unwittingly revealed much later on at the time when he began to complain and to curse the day of his birth. Please note Chapter 3, verses 25 and 26 (Darby):

> *For I feared a fear, and it hath come upon me,*
> *And that which I dreaded hath come to me.*
> *I was not in safety, neither had I quietness,*
> *neither was I at rest,*
> *And trouble came.*

Does not this secret apprehension disclose that the knowledge of God in Job was imperfect? He knew the Lord, as he confessed much later (42.5), only by hearing. He had yet to know Him by seeing. Yes, he feared God. Yes, he was protected and blessed by God. He even had the presence and the guidance and the illumination that came from God. Yet all the while there was a profound dread within Job from which he could not escape.

What did he fear? What was he afraid of? He was afraid as to how long this blessed state could continue. "I have tried my best to serve God; I have asserted my utmost effort to abstain from evil; and because of that, the Lord has blessed me, prospered me, and given me peace. But how long can I remain in such a state? Suppose I slip? What, *then,* will happen to me? Will He continue to bless me? Will He still protect me and prosper me?"

Although Job had advanced a certain distance, even so, he never felt safe and secure. There was always a hidden secret dread lurking within him: True, I am blessed by God at *this* moment, but what about tomorrow? He lived and served before God in constant fear and trembling: "I was not in safety, neither had I quietness, neither was I at rest." Although he loved the Lord with a perfect heart, he had not yet reached that stage of utter abandonment toward Him. He did not have that rest in God. In short, his was a restless soul. "And trouble came" to him at last—the trouble he had so greatly feared. So that in spite of his perfect heart there was much still to be done in that life. Nevertheless, must we not confess how amazing it is to see that even with his rather limited knowledge of God, Job could still be such a perfect man?

❦

BEFORE WE GO ON, however, perhaps we need to apply this picture of Job to ourselves. Let us suppose that, like him, we are not beginners. Let us suppose we have believed in the Lord for some time and have gone on with Him for a while. Moreover, suppose we have a perfect heart toward God, that we know what is righteousness—that is, Christ is our righteousness. And suppose we not only fear God but we even love Him, because the love of Christ has constrained us. Suppose, too, that we abstain from evil; and more than this, we do the things which are righteous in the sight of God. Even suppose further that we live under the protection of God, that we know the guidance of the Lord, that we are being illuminated by Him and have been initiated into His mysteries. We have progressed so well in being taught of God that we are even able to instruct and to help others also.

In such circumstances as these, it will be obvious to anyone that we are not a novice. It must readily be acknowledged that we have grown out of our spiritual babyhood. But can it automatically be said that we have grown into adulthood? Too often, because we have gone a certain distance with the Lord, it is very easy to delude ourselves into thinking we have reached maturity—spiritual adulthood. We will think, as did Job: These are the days of my autumn—these are days of my spiritual maturity. For you are being respected; you are being admired; you seem to have much; and you seem to be able to give much.

Like Job, though, we are terribly deceived if because of this we conclude we have reached the highest level of maturity. What then *is* our spiritual state? In actuality, we find we are neither in the state of babyhood nor in the state of adulthood. We are in that in-between stage

35

known as spiritual adolescence. If we can see this, it perhaps can explain a number of things.

You know, a person who is in his adolescence tends to think he knows everything. And this is what we so often are like, not only in the natural realm but especially when it comes to our spiritual walk. If we are newly saved and freshly born of the Spirit of God, we *know* that we know nothing. Humility is just natural to us then because in very fact we *do* know nothing. But, the real problem arises after we have reached a certain spiritual plateau—at which plane we can often become deceived because we believe have arrived. Whereas most often in truth, we are but in the stage of adolescence: we are still on the way.

Yes it is true, on the one hand, we cannot say we do not know anything or we do not have any spiritual experience. We cannot honestly say we do not know the Lord or that we are not under His divine illumination. We as a matter of fact have all these things. Nevertheless, it is equally true that we do not have in our heart that rest—that utter repose—in God. We do not feel safe and secure in our heart. There is, instead, a secret hidden fear there, which is, Am I really safe? As long as I please God, yes He gives me peace and prospers my way; but what if I should slip? What about tomorrow?

Dear friend, are you as Job, still restless in your heart? Do you feel unsafe and insecure? Or is there an absolute abandonment to God and to His will? Do you know a rest wherein you rest from all your labors as God has rested from all His (Heb. 4.10; cf. Ex. 20.11)? Or is it that all your spiritual attainment is more a matter of your own effort than a real abandonment to

God? What, dear one, is your spiritual state? If you are in the same condition as Job, self-deceived into presuming you have arrived at the days of your autumn, then you will find there is something further the Lord has to do in order to bring you into real maturity. He has to bring in one crisis or another, and through these crises He will mature you into true spirituality. And this is exactly the point in the history of Job we have now reached, what is presently before us. For suddenly, without any warning, the scene is abruptly shifted. God is about to bring in the crisis.

INSTEAD OF THE EARTH, as was found in Chapter 1 and verse 5, the scene in verse 6 is immediately shifted to heaven. Keep in mind, though, that this is *not* the third heaven (see Paul's testimony in 2 Cor. 12.2; cf. also Eph. 4.10, Heb. 4.14) from which Satan had been cast out. This is not the heaven of heavens where God set his throne eternally and dwells permanently. How do we know this? Because Satan had once been cast out from *that* realm, never to return (cf. Is. 14.12ff. and Ez. 28, esp. v.14ff.).

Anyway, here is a scene which is not on the earth but somewhere in the heavenly realm. And what is shown is the Lord God holding a court. Sometimes a writer of the Scriptures, when attempting to describe something, has to do so in a way we his readers can understand. And hence we have this scene before us of God holding as it were a circuit court. From time to time His angelic messengers or emissaries will report to Him everything they have noticed and observed on the earth concerning mankind.

Do we realize we are being reported on, and not by any earthly FBI but by heavenly angels? God sends His ministering spirits to minister especially to those who know the redemption of the Lord, and from time to time He awaits his messengers to report back to Him. And it was on one such occasion as this, when God's emissaries returned to report to Him about this one and that one and about this thing and that thing, that Satan was found among them. He was allowed to come to this court to be an accuser. We know that Satan has another name—the Accuser of the brethren (Rev. 12.10). He always tries to accuse us before God. And it was on one of these days when God's angelic servants appeared before His presence to give an account of their findings that Satan appeared too.

We Christians need to understand that man does not live alone. If man were left on the earth by himself many things that *do* happen would not occur at all. Yet we do not live on earth all by ourselves, because this passage in JOB uncovers the very important fact that man is the center of a conflict between God and His adversary Satan: God wants man, but Satan wants him too. God wants to perfect man that he may be conformed to the image of His beloved Son, but Satan wants to destroy man that man may share in Satan's eternal doom. God wants to use man to defeat His enemy and to fulfill His purpose through man that He may receive praise and glory and honor from man, but

Satan tries to discredit God through man.

Hence man is not left alone to direct his own destiny. He is not entirely free to go his own way. Far from it, he has become the target of both the Almighty and Satan. But has not man been created as such—as a controversial personality? He has been created by God for the purpose of defeating His enemy. And thus Satan makes man his main target of attack. He is all the time attempting to resist and to frustrate God by enticing man into an unholy alliance with him. And hence man is caught in the center of a great spiritual conflict.

Yet such conflict is to be expected and not to be surprised at by us. It is clear that without this piece of information we will be thrown into confusion whenever we are subjected to trials. There are so many things we simply cannot explain if this bit of knowledge is lacking. But if we know there is a heavenly combat such as this raging, then many unexplainable matters turn out to be understandable. Do remember this one thing: that we, far from living on earth by ourselves, are caught up in a tremendous clash, a battle which is much bigger than man, an issue larger than any problem man has. And this explains why the scene in JOB was changed so drastically and so suddenly by being shifted from earth to heaven where, as we have seen, God was holding his circuit court and where, too, Satan suddenly appeared.

HOWEVER, BEFORE Satan could commence his work of

accusation, God first challenged him. I hope you can grasp the significance of this point. God was not one to wait until Satan began to accuse, since that would have put Him on the defensive. No, it was God who took the initiative—by challenging His enemy with Job. This is an important matter for us to see. It was not through the accusation of Satan by which Job entered into his severe trials; quite the reverse, it was the challenge of the Lord that precipitated the whole course which plunged him into deep waters. *God himself commenced the entire affair.* But of course without Job's knowledge.

Thus we find the Lord challenging His adversary with this man Job. He was the pride of God and the envy of Satan. The Lord had so much confidence in him that He could challenge His enemy with him, because He knew Job more than Job knew himself and He knew Job more than Satan knew Job. Praise the Lord! He will not permit us to be tried above what we are able to bear, but He will, with the trial, bring forth a living issue (see 1 Cor. 10.13 Darby).

Brothers and sisters, do we think we are in such a position that God can dare take us up and challenge Satan with us and say, Have you noticed my servant so-and-so? Most likely with many of us He would try His best to cover us lest we be accused. If there is any person on this earth whom God can take up and use to challenge Satan with, what a blessed position that one has attained.

Let us therefore understand and ever keep in mind that in a certain sense all the troubles and everything else which followed were initiated by God alone. He himself is the explanation for all which came upon Job.

But why did God do this? Is it that He merely desired to show off to Satan and thus put Job into great trouble? Yet if He simply wanted to show him off to Satan, then how utterly miserable He made the life of His servant as a consequence. No, it was not a matter of God's showing off, for He does not enjoy seeing His people suffer. It was because He had a definite purpose in mind concerning Job. God knew His servant and knew precisely what He was doing. What He was doing was simply *using* Satan to complete His own work in that man.

FOR MANY YEARS I had had trouble with JOB. As I studied this book I just could not understand why all these things. Is it a story which has as its purpose to teach us the mystery of suffering: how suffering can work something positive into a life? What exactly is it which this narrative is trying to show us? What is God attempting to tell us? Over a very long period I tried to find out before the Lord, until one day that interesting verse in James 5 brought light to me: "Behold, we call them blessed that endured: ye have heard of the endurance of Job, and have seen the end of the Lord, how that the Lord is full of pity, and merciful" (v.11 mg.).

Ye have heard of the endurance of Job. Some versions render it the *patience* of Job, but actually there is a difference between the two. Patience is toward persons, endurance is toward things. Thus it is more accurately the endurance of Job. He endured all these troubles, all these sufferings, all these sicknesses, and all these deprivations. God's servant endured.

Our attention is easily caught by that, is it not? As we read through JOB we are drawn to the drama of this man's endurance. How he endured all these circumstances. And our response is: "Lord, enable *me* to endure. Oh that I too may endure!" We do thank God for Job's endurance of these many things, and for the lesson his experience can teach us. We truly need to learn the same lesson. Sometimes we suffer a little bit, we are being deprived somewhat; but then we commence to murmur and complain and finally to rebel. How we need to experience the endurance of Job in our lives.

Yet I do not believe Job's endurance is the chief lesson of this book. That is but the story, the surface of things. It is only a by-product; it is not the main concern of the narrative. For please observe that the endurance of Job only tells us what is going on, it does not tell us *unto what*. To what purpose is it all? True, Job endured a great deal of suffering; and this is the process. But you do not go through a process without coming forth with the end-product. Hence we must ask ourselves, Why the process? What is the final product in view? The very next phrase in James 5.11 gives the answer: The process of endurance is because there is "the end of the Lord". The Lord has an "end" in view.

End means purpose; it also means the very last, the final thing; which is therefore to say, that God's purpose—the finality of the Lord—is fulfilled, is realized.

Finally—through these many trials and sufferings, through all the misunderstandings and persecutions, through all these various enemies—finally, the end of the Lord is seen. God has at last gotten what He first set out to do.

The "end of the Lord" is thus the key to JOB. This first book of the sacred record has been included to show us the eternal purpose of God concerning mankind. Why was man created? Why does he suffer? Does man suffer because he has sinned? Will he always be prosperous if he does not sin? What is it that God is really after in man? and in this man Job particularly? Why is it that He allows these circumstances to come upon this man? Is there a purpose, a meaning behind it all? As God put Job through the process did a final product emerge? What essentially *is* the end of the Lord?

Read the concluding chapter of the book and you will discover the end of the Lord to be that *Job received a double portion.* The Lord doubled his possessions. God took away, that He might double it. Job's loss was Job's gain or, may we say, Job's loss was God's gain. Accordingly, the end and purpose of the Lord is a double portion. But what exactly is meant, you may wonder, by this phrase? Briefly stated, it is *sonship.* It is the birthright and the blessing of the firstborn son. The double portion, as our discussion of the last chapter of JOB will more fully show, is merely a pictorial way of saying: Here is sonship—spiritual maturity—finally arrived at.

Consequently, the lesson to be found in this book is the lesson of sonship. Sonship in the Scriptures is a very big matter. Literally speaking, it means "the placing of sons"—which is to say, that a person, having reached a certain maturity, is to be placed publicly as son, as heir, as collaborator or joint partaker of the father. When at first we are born again, we are but children. We need to grow up into sonship, into the full purpose of our Father-God.

Now in one sense Job is superior to us believers, for we see him as perfect and righteous, fearing God and abstaining from evil. He has reached quite a moral position before the Lord. In another sense, however, we are more privileged than Job, for *Christ* has become our righteousness, and we are constrained by the love of Christ rather than knowing only the fear of God. So that we may consider it rather generally that the first appearance of Job in the story can serve as a type or illustration of us Christians today in the beginning stage of spiritual life.

We, like the early Job, serve the Lord with a more or less perfect heart. We are reckoned as righteous before God and men. So far as we know we abstain from evil and learn to walk in the fear of God. Yet as Paul in the Galatian letter makes clear, the child is not much different from the slave: "But I say that so long as the heir is a child, he differeth nothing from a bondservant though he is lord of all; but is under guardians and stewards until the day appointed of the father" (4.1–2). Too often, our childish thought, as was Job's, is: If we continually serve the Lord we will be blessed with prosperity and peace. We therefore live in constant apprehension lest one day we offend God and thus be punished with poverty, sickness, or deprivation. Such an immature outlook has to undergo a change. God is not satisfied to have us merely as children. He has to mature us into sons. But such maturing is a painful process. It is the pain of growth. Now if we want to avoid the pain, we at the same time will avoid growth. But if we want to grow, we will have to go through pain. Such is the maturing of the sons of God. But such, too, is the end of the Lord. The Lord's desire is that we may be blessed not only as children but more so as sons of God who will be heirs and co-heirs with Christ.

Yet this passage in James 5 further indicates that the Lord is full of tender compassion and merciful. Is not this observation of James' rather strange? For as you read through Job do you not almost come to the same conclusion which Job did at one time?—that God is harsh to me, He is cruel, He is determined to crush me, He does not care (see 30.18ff.). That will always be the case if we look only at the beginning of the suffering process: we will quite naturally think that the Lord is a most cruel and hardhearted God: He allows people to suffer and seems to enjoy it.

But when you see to the very end of the Lord, you know you have misunderstood Him. Far from being harsh and cruel and without care in the process, He is full of pity and mercy. Seeing God's end, your whole understanding of Him is changed. You have a new and better comprehension of Him and of His ways. You realize you now have God completely. You come to discern that even in the stripping, it is still His love—He is still full of tender compassion and merciful.

I do not know how you feel, but to me I feel that all this of which James 5.11 speaks is the central thought

45

and lesson to be seen in the book of Job, and which explains everything which happened to this man as he was put into the crucible of suffering. It was all unto the purpose of maturity, unto the end of sonship. The Lord was not satisfied with Job; to Him he was still a child, not yet a son. His entire outlook, so far as God saw things, was still immature; it was not yet fully grown. Because of this, and although Job was by this time already the pride of God and the envy of Satan, the Lord's hand had to come upon him in a new way. Having seen a potential in His servant, God in His love and mercy was determined to bring it to perfection, even if it meant grievous suffering for Job. He still had something more to do with this man, and out of that desire He challenged Satan with him.

AT THE TIME of the Lord's challenge concerning His servant, God first asked His enemy: "What have you been doing? From where have you come?" And Satan's reply was: "From going to and fro in the earth, and from walking up and down in it" (1.7). Is this not characteristic of the Adversary? He is continually going everywhere, and going about very hastily. He is rushing here and rushing there, trying to find something with which he can frustrate God and destroy man. Has not Peter rightly said that our adversary the devil, as a roaring lion, walks about, seeking to devour whomsoever he can? (1 Peter 5.8)

46

Next, though, God inquired of Satan further: "Have you noticed my servant Job?" Of course Satan had noticed him! And God knew this too. He knew that Job had been the target of Satan's intense observation. The latter must have thought many times to attack him, because if he could destroy this man he could bring disgrace to God. But he could not attack Job since God had hedged him in. God had indeed put a protective shield around Job. And around his family and possessions too. The enemy could not do anything to him without the Lord's permission. And thank God for that! The Bible clearly declares that we will not be tempted or tried above what we are able to bear because everything is in God's hand (see 1 Cor. 10.13). Do not be afraid, therefore. Satan cannot do anything, because we are mercifully hedged in by the Lord.

But the Adversary then began to make accusation. It was a false and vicious attack on Job, since he attempted to ascribe a base motive to him. Said Satan, Yes, I have noticed Job. Yes, it is true that he is perfect, is upright, fears God, and abstains from evil. I acknowledge all that; but there is a reason for it: it is because You have hedged him in: You have protected him and blessed him: You have prospered him by giving him sons and daughters, possessions and properties. Of course he fears You! But suppose You take away the hedge. Suppose he loses everything he has. If that happens, he will *curse* You to Your very face!

Satan, in other words, does not and can not and will not believe that there is such a thing as an unselfish love, a disinterested love, a pure love for God. To him it is impossible, and he is so obsessed by this that he

47

believes in his own lie. The Accuser tries to lay a mean and base motive to everything. And why? Because he measures all things by the measurement of himself. We know, do we not, that this is how that angel of light Lucifer became the fallen angel Satan? (cf. Is. 14.12 AV)—he served God for nothing but gain, and when he could obtain nothing by such service, he hated God and rebelled against Him. He never does anything out of an unselfish motive. For to him there *is* no unselfish thing. To him, there is no such thing as disinterested love. Why should people love God? Only for themselves— only for self-profit, is Satan's reasoning. If people do not gain anything they will not love God. To him, everybody is wholly out for profit and selfish purpose.

Consequently, Satan explains everything by himself. And because this is the kind of being he is—selfish and self-centered to the core—he automatically assumed that Job too was selfish in his fearing and serving God. Satan just cannot believe that Job—a man who, as all other men, is made only a little lower than an angel like himself—can love God unselfishly. Although he had observed the perfectness of Job, he would not accept it at its face value. He would instead impute a base reason to account for such a noble life: it is personal gain, and nothing else, which motivates a man to fear God. But allow all of a man's blessings to fade away and he will curse God to His face. How so characteristic of Satan this accusation itself is: because he could not gain what he wanted himself, therefore he cursed God and later became His adversary. And hence Satan simply could not conceive of anyone else acting otherwise; with the

48

result that he brought forth this false accusation against the Lord's servant.

❧

GOD HAD TO take up this accusation. Said He, "All right, I will take away the hedge. You can do anything you like with what he has; except that upon himself you are not to put forth your hand." And having thus obtained the Lord's permission, Satan went out and performed his masterpiece of diabolical destruction. In just one day all Job's possessions were laid waste; even all his children—the apples of his eye—were wiped out. Relentlessly, out of nowhere, came disaster after disaster after disaster. A spiritual crisis of immense proportions had descended upon Job.

It must be borne in mind that by this time Job had lived a long while on the earth. Some commentators believe he was 70 years old; others say, more likely 100 years. The magnitude of such a catastrophe to this desert prince can therefore hardly be reckoned. All that he had accumulated over the years—both through perhaps diligent efforts on his part, and of course by the blessing of God—vanished from before his eyes in a single day. He was left with nothing.

Just here we need to remind ourselves of a very important distinction that should be made, which is, that although God had undeniably initiated the crisis, it was not He himself who had attacked Job. It is quite true that God's challenge to Satan was what had plunged Job into deep waters, but the unmerciful attack upon His servant had come from another quarter: it was the Lord's enemy who had wielded the sword. This distinction should not be lost sight of lest we unwarrantedly attribute evil to God.

And what was this man's response to the attack? Listen to how the Scriptures describe it:

> *Then Job arose, and rent his robe, and shaved his head, and fell down upon the ground, and worshipped; and he said, Naked came I out of my mother's womb, and naked shall I return thither: Jehovah gave, and Jehovah hath taken away; blessed be the name of Jehovah. In all this Job sinned not, nor charged God foolishly.* (1.20–22)

Throughout this unusual trial, Job did not ascribe anything unseemly toward the Lord, for here was a man who loved God with an unselfish, disinterested, and pure love. The Lord knew it was there: it only needed to be brought out. He knew that deep down in the heart of this servant of His there was such a love toward Him; but of course, there were impurities too. These impurities—unknown to Job—needed to be purified in order that the pure love toward God that had been planted in him by His grace might be brought out and manifested.

THE CRISIS DID NOT CEASE, however. Another day came

to pass, because although the enemy was defeated in the first test he would not give up the assault. But once again, God challenged him with Job by saying: "He still holdeth fast his integrity, although thou movedst me against him, to swallow him up without cause" (2.3 mg.). But Satan pressed the attack by retorting: "Skin for skin, yea, all that a man hath will he give for his life" (2.4). You have not touched his life yet, said Satan; a man is willing to give up everything to preserve his own life. So the enemy in return challenged God with this: "Put forth thy hand now, and touch his bone and his flesh, and he will renounce thee to thy face" (2.5). The Lord therefore said to him, All right, you can *touch* his life but do not take *away* his life.

And we know the result: Job was afflicted with a grievous botch; from head to foot he was filled with sores. It was an extremely hideous and painful kind of disease called elephant leprosy because the feet are known to swell at times to the size of an elephant's. His whole body was covered with the ghastly plague.

Job now became a castaway. He could not remain at home, but had to go out of the city to the dung heap where the people burned their refuse. He was reduced to one of the most miserable conditions imaginable. There he sat among the ashes, with the outcasts and the beggars as his companions, and scraped his wounds with a potsherd. Even his wife could not abide his condition anymore, but taunted him to his face and said: "Dost thou still remain firm in thine integrity? curse God and die"! (2.9 Darby) She was unconsciously used by Satan to tempt her own husband to curse the Lord. Yet once again Job did not rebel against God, for he said:

"What? shall we receive good at the hand of God, and shall we not receive evil?" (2.10)

In spite of all the unexpected calamities which befell him, Job did not sin with his lips against the Lord. He was willing to submit himself to the government of God. He did not understand; nonetheless he would accept whatever God apportioned to him. He recognized that the Lord had a right to give and to take away. And he was ready to accept evil as well as good from Him, even though prior to the coming of the crisis he had been living in continual dread lest one day his God-blessed life were altered by evil trouble or trial. And thus do we see that he was not really as according to Satan's accusation of loving the Lord with ulterior motive, consciously loving the blessings of God more than God himself. Not so. Job *did* love God, despite the fact that by all outward appearances he had seemed to do so out of self-interest. All which was needed was for the pure love within him to be brought out under the pressure of circumstances. And this very thing the crisis had done. It was now proven fully that Job did not fear God because of personal gain. He feared and served Him solely out of love. So that Satan was at last silenced.

HERE, THEN, is the crisis: we have been beholding a man who when tested was able to stand before God and Satan and to love God with an unselfish and pure love.

Yet all who follow the Lord will themselves someday come into a similar spiritual crisis. All who serve Him will one day be tested on this very matter of love. Do we love God with an unselfish, disinterested and pure sort or do we love Him because He has blessed us? Suppose God were to strip *you* of everything? Would you still love Him? Suppose evil circumstances come upon you, will you still maintain your integrity before Him? Sooner or later in our spiritual life such a testing will come, such a principle of God's dealing with His children will most surely come upon us.

In what manner, though, is such a principle to be applied? We must realize that what is shown to us in this narrative is only the divine principle, with Job's life as but an illustration of that principle. Whether the testing comes once, or twice, or many times does not really matter. The principle nonetheless runs throughout. But as to the application of the principle in each Christian's experience, this is something which is up to the Spirit of God to decide.

What I am trying to do in this study of Job is to describe one man's spiritual experience. But because it *is* spiritual experience, we therefore cannot generalize, we cannot be too rigid. True, in our spiritual experiences we can in fact find some principle or principles, but their application to our lives is in the hands of the Holy Spirit. We cannot make divine principles so fixed, but on the contrary their application to us must be left to the wisdom of God's Spirit.

So how do you come into such crises? Only the Lord knows the character and timing of such circumstances. It is something not arranged by man but is a matter known only to God. To have it otherwise will be disastrous. He alone knows the timing. He will not allow you to enter this experience of testing before you are ready. He knows you far better than you yourself do. Knowing your heart as He does, God will not allow you to be tempted above what you can bear—that is, what His grace within you is able to take (cf. 1 Cor. 10.13). Only at the right moment will He challenge Satan with you, but when that moment does arrive it becomes a testing—a crisis—in your spiritual life.

YET REMEMBER THAT God's purpose in the crisis is something quite glorious: it is to bring out of our hearts what His grace has already put within of His pure love. God has already done this work of grace in us; He well knows it; but within us it is being covered, it is being mixed with impurities of which we are not aware. But out of such a crisis, that which is impure in us will be revealed. Yet thank God, too, that that which is pure in us will also be brought out into greater glory. We ought to be purified and become purer than ever. And this is precisely what the Lord's purpose was to be in the case of Job and his crisis.

O God our Father, we bow our hearts before You in love and adoration. We marvel at Your wisdom. How You precipitate crises in our lives that You may purify us. Your desire is to bring many sons into glory. Teach us how to submit ourselves to Your hand and to be wholly abandoned to Your will. Let us not question Your wisdom, but let us ever put our trust in You. Forgive us if we waver. Yet do not let go Your hand upon us until Your glorious design is perfected. Thank You, O Father, for Your patience with us. We pray in the name of Your Son our Lord Jesus Christ. Amen.

PART TWO

The Searching of the Soul

Remember, I pray thee, who ever perished, being innocent?
  They that plow iniquity, and sow mischief, reap the same:
By the breath of God they perish.

  If thou return to the Almighty, thou shalt be built up,
If thou put away unrighteousness far from thy tents.
                    —ELIPHAZ THE TEMANITE

Behold, God will not cast away a perfect man,
  Neither will he uphold the evildoers.

If thou wert pure and upright:
  Surely now God would awake for thee,
And make the habitation of thy righteousness prosperous.
                    —BILDAD THE SHUHITE

Knowest thou not this of old time,
  That the triumphing of the wicked is short,
And the joy of the godless but for a moment?

  But thou sayest, My doctrine is pure,
And I am clean in thine eyes.
    Know therefore that God exacteth of thee less than thine iniquity deserveth.
                    —ZOPHAR THE NAAMATHITE

Ye are forgers of lies;
  Ye are all physicians of no value.

How long will ye vex my soul,
  And break me in pieces with words?
These ten times have ye reproached me:
  Ye are not ashamed that ye deal hardly with me.

Have pity upon me, have pity upon me, O ye my friends;
  For the hand of God hath touched me.

Oh that I knew where I might find God!
  That I might come even to his seat!
I would set my cause in order before him,
  And understand what he would say unto me.
But I cannot behold him;
  He hideth himself that I cannot see him.
                    —JOB THE SERVANT OF GOD

The Searching of the Soul

THE BEAUTY of a flower. Such is the apt phrase one commentator has used to describe Job's life before his nest had been so dramatically disturbed. For his had been a life that, like a flower, had been most beautiful and attractive, much to be admired and appreciated. Yet there is a difference between the beauty of a flower and the beauty of its fruit. One may behold a flower's lovely form and color in terms of aesthetic beauty, but that is not something which, practically speaking, can benefit the beholder. Only the fruit of the flower can truly satisfy. In order to bear its fruit, however, it must one day be shorn of its outward beauty: its petals must fall, leaving the flower quite bare. Nevertheless, out of such barrenness there comes forth the fruit. And it is the fruit which the flower's Creator is ultimately after. For only the fruit of the flower can genuinely satisfy the hungry.

We may therefore say that Job's life at the beginning of the Bible narrative has been depicted to us as a very beautiful plant. He was one to be admired and appreciated and respected greatly, both by God and man. And yet God desired something further. He desired that Job might become a fruit. And because of this, the petals of the flower of Job's beauty and attractiveness had to be stripped away. However, out of such barrenness and brokenness there will emerge a fruitful, matured life, one which shall bring glory to God and satisfaction to man.

This, in a sense, is the whole story of the life of Job. As he continued to be prospered and blessed by the hand of God, there was in his heart on the one hand a hope—a fervent expectation that he would rest forever in his nest. On the other hand, there was also a secret fear that this kind of peaceful and bountiful way might not continue. And one day that fear and that dread became a reality. His nest was totally destroyed. The petals of Job's beauty were unceremoniously shorn away.

Not by degrees *but in just one day* God stripped His servant of everything. All seven sons and all three daughters, the pride of Job and the envious respect of the populace, vanished like a passing vapor. All his possessions—the cattle and sheep which provided him food and clothing, the camels and she-asses which gave him the means of distant and local transport, the oxen which worked his many fields, and the maids and servants who were his workmen—all these possessions which had served Job so well and had made him so great in the eyes of men were totally annihilated. His standing before the people and in the community was rudely and utterly shattered. This man, this spiritual man if you please, was left literally naked before God and humanity. Said he, "Naked I came, and naked I shall return." The soul of Job was laid starkly bare. And this was the crisis we earlier saw.

At this point, though, we need to stop for a moment and apply to ourselves the fuller significance of what has just been said. Spiritually speaking, I believe, we can say that a man's *sons and daughters* can represent his various spiritual virtues and fruits, because a man's children are his offspring: they come out from himself and are therefore his fruit. They tell us *what he is*. By viewing the children we know who and what kind of father this man is. Hence in spiritual terms we can consider sons and daughters as representing the man himself, what he is both before God and people. They strengthen his hand and beautify his life. Out of his walk with the Lord, and through his seeking and searching and effort, there emerge certain qualities which appear quite prominent. He is therefore a man full of virtue and full of strength. And such a man is proud of such spiritual offspring and tries hard to make them acceptable to God.

The *possessions* of a man, on the other hand—and in Job's case, they were his cattle and sheep, his camels, oxen, and asses, his maids and servants, houses and fields—represent *what he has;* that is to say, what a person has accumulated through the years. Applying these possessions spiritually, may it not be said that through the years we believers have not only accumulated some virtues but have also amassed a great deal of knowledge, truth, experiences, works, and so forth? They seem to serve us so well in our spiritual life and to make us great in the sight of men.

Oh dear friends, what for sure will make you and me great in the eyes of man? Well, if we exhibit such spiritual virtues or bear such spiritual fruits as love, joy, peace, long-suffering, kindliness, self-control, and so on, then that will make us great. Moreover, if we possess certain accomplishments—such as spiritual knowledge, works, and experience—these too will make us great in man's sight. Yet sooner or later all these must be swept away.

It is very true that as we follow the Lord He will add virtue after virtue to us. It is very true that out of our life with the Lord we will increasingly gather knowledge and there will continually be works done by us: and all these will make us loom large in the view of God and in the view of man. But this so-called knowledge and these so-called works are quite often a great mixture. We cannot say there is no work of the Holy Spirit in it; nonetheless, we must acknowledge that much of it is the result of our own efforts. We cannot say there is nothing spiritual surrounding it; even so, we have to confess that a great deal of it remains in the soulish realm. There has yet to be a time when the spirit and the soul are *divided* (Heb. 4.12), and the way to enter into such an experience is for our soul, as was Job's, to be stripped naked.

Brethren, we will never know our soul until first it is stripped naked before God. If we are in possession of all our sons and daughters and all our vast accumulations— that is to say, if we have all our virtues and all our works, experience, and knowledge—we are just not able to penetrate to the depths of our soul and to know it. Such adornment too often generates a false sense of spirituality, causing us to feel we have arrived some-where and even conceivably deceiving us into believing we have arrived at the very end. For this reason God has first of all to allow all these beauties of the flower to be blown away, and as we are in a state of nakedness before Him we like Job shall experience a deep soul searching and we shall be thoroughly found out. We shall commence to know, as did he, what is really within our soul.

Now WE MUST note that as Job was cast into this awesome crisis he was quite able, *at the beginning,* to stand up victoriously. Had he not quietly affirmed: "Naked I came, and naked I return; God gives, and God takes away; blessed be the name of the Lord"? When tested to the uttermost Job could courageously assert, "Shall we not receive evil, even as we have received good, from God?" How firm, how strong, how spiritual he was. In spite of his every weakness he was able to stand undaunted for God and to remain true to the Lord. He was able to demonstrate a disinterested and pure love toward his God. So that Satan's accusation proved wholly to be false. The enemy was defeated and the enemy was silenced. But God was honored.

Yet there is a most remarkable facet to all of this which should not go unnoticed by us. We must not forget that the trial of adversity had come upon Job very swiftly and most unexpectedly. No intimation of what was to come had been given him whatsoever. We must therefore take note of the fact that God's servant at the beginning had had no time to pause and reflect.

Because everything had engulfed him so suddenly, he had not had the slightest chance to consider. And as a consequence we find that he responded almost automatically—in fact, quite spontaneously—to what had befallen him. But in view of this, we need to ask ourselves how it was possible for Job, on the spur of the moment, to manifest such a modest, humble and submissive reaction to what was admittedly a most profound crisis. How are we to explain the admirable manner in which Job initially conducted himself as he underwent such intense fire?

If you will but consider this matter for a moment I believe you will readily agree that if anyone says something following a time of reflection such an utterance does not really represent that person. Whereas what comes out of a person on the spur of the moment betrays what he truly is. And if this be the case, then what did Job's instant and unconscious reaction to an unexpected trial reveal about *his* inward condition? Must it not be acknowledged that the kind of spontaneous response which he exhibited was of God himself in Job? Yes, there is no question but what this that we have seen in him was the true Job coming forth. No doubt about it. And what a beautiful thing it was. Yet such a marvelous display of spiritual nobility—both in humble speech and submissive act—was indisputably the work of God's grace in that man. Over the years God had wrought deeply in His servant. And hence Job's immediate reaction in the face of such enormous and relentless pressure reveals that there was resident within him *at the beginning* of his trial a considerable spiritual reserve. And out of that reservoir of God's grace Job was able to withstand the enemy assault so nobly and to stand up so triumphantly. And this is the explanation, it seems to me, for the sturdy and godly quality which characterized the unthinking response he made to the crisis.

But please realize, dear friends, that this spiritual reserve is not inexhaustible. Yes, Job was able to withstand the harshest attacks of the enemy, but we shall discover that when his three friends come to comfort him he will have searched the very bottom of his soul. We shall then witness in him quite a different reaction to that which he exhibited at the first. A *counter* response will have then set in. And this we shall take note of presently.

As WAS EARLIER indicated, we do believe that Job is a real person. But then too we believe that his three friends are real people. What is recorded in JOB is a narrative which for the most part has been set down in poetic form; nevertheless, what the entire narrative is concerned with are real facts, real persons, real events. And in the particular section of JOB now before us, it is no different. In designating Chapters 3 to 31 as The Searching of the Soul of Job, we accept what is recorded there as being quite true, that it is something which happened historically. A discussion is going on among these three friends and Job. Debates take place, weighty arguments are exchanged, and words become heated.

The entire event, we shall find, is most interesting, and its outcome to Job devastating.

But right here, may I suggest a way for us to read these chapters? I would like to present the whole of it in allegorical or parabolical form. By parabolical form or parable I do not mean to imply, to repeat again, that what is set down here is not true and real, because as a matter of fact this is not the implication of Job's use of the word parable either. For it will be observed that this very part of the narrative now under discussion twice records that Job "again took up his parable" and continued on with it, and yet his very parable related to his own real experience (see both 27.1 and 29.1).

No, what I mean by parable is this. I would like to present these chapters in the form of a naked soul as it stands before God and goes through a time of deep searchings. The words of Job and the words of his companions can represent what takes place far down within a man's soul. The voice of Job and the voices of the friends are the voices of a man's inner depths. He muses within himself. He argues and debates with himself. Many various, even contrary, things occur deep inside him. His soul, now naked, is being searched out under the light of God. Whether that makes any sense to you or not I do not know. But it does make sense to me: a soul that, having been laid bare before God, experiences a profound searching and in the process is being found out. So that in one respect it can be said that the many rounds of debate between Job and his three friends can very well represent what is going on deeply within Job himself.

⚜

To PROCEED with such a presentation as this, however, we must turn ahead to Chapter 30. For if you are to feel the full impact of what is going on inside Job you will have to compare Chapter 29, already discussed previously, with Chapter 30.

You will recall that in Chapter 29 Job tried to tell us what a resplendent life he lived in those days of prosperity when the Lord so wonderfully preserved him. A life of enlightenment, of illumination; a life full of good works and high esteem; a life he thought he could go on with restfully and successfully to the very end of his days. Yet hidden away within him was a secret dread: Job feared it might not be so.

Turn to Chapter 30, however, and you are struck by an entirely opposite picture. There Job has become a derisive song of all the people. Especially has he become a byword to the young ones and to those whom he had known previously as outcasts. He is a marked man, despised and rejected by everybody. They abhor him, and do not spare to spit in his face nor to push him around and kick him about. Moreover, by his having become a companion of the ostrich and a friend of the jackal, his skin has become black from the continual exposure to the sun and his bones are burned with its heat. How days of grievous affliction have truly taken hold of Job; his soul is being poured out like water. Someone, in fact, has suggested that it is nearly comparable to a picture of the suffering of our Lord Jesus. If you were to compare Chapter 30 very closely with some of the verses in the Messianic Psalms which relate how the Lord later is to suffer you would indeed discover such parallels all along the way.

What does it mean? It simply means the cross. Here is a person who is stripped of everything and is going through a period of darkness. Yet if God will remain with him, if only God will make it clear that He is with him, then he can bear all these things. But he cannot find God. He simply cannot. On the contrary, he is shut off from Him (see 23.3–9). And as a consequence he becomes confused. Puzzled. Perplexed. Now some people would like to call this the dark night of the soul. But it may also be termed the deeper working of the cross. And it is as a person is put under a circumstance like this that he begins to fathom the true condition of his soul.

WITH THIS AS a background, then, let us turn to Job's present situation and the three friends who have come to see him. Previously we saw that Satan had been silenced in his attacks upon Job. In fact we do not find his presence any further in the narrative. But can we say he is altogether dismissed from the scene? I am afraid he is still there, but now with hidden tactics in mind. He had failed in his earlier attacks, but hereafter he will try another yet more subtle artifice. He will use sympathy and concern instead of direct assaults. And as we shall soon learn, Satan almost succeeded. As I said, we no longer see him, but we do see from this moment onward the three friends. They shall be able to disturb the peace of Job which all the prior calamities could never have done. How often, like Job, we are able to withstand the blatant assault of the enemy, but the reaction which comes in afterward, through such reflection and interior activity as Job's three friends subtly induce, are nearly too much for us. It is far easier to stand against the enemy attack than against the well-meaning intentions of our closest friends.

So here came Job's three companions. They were not only his friends, they were his best friends: they loved him very much, even as their very own soul. For they came from great distances. And they came with the purpose of comforting him. But before they had reached the site they had talked among themselves, since they had obviously come to a common agreement even before they arrived (cf. 2.11b). And as they drew near and beheld Job sitting in the dunghill among the ashes they could not even recognize him. How a prince had fallen! They "saw that his grief was very great"—so great, in fact, that they could not open their mouth; they simply sat with him seven days and seven nights in utter silence (2.13).

Can we not see from this the greatness of the trial? the depths of the agony? Job could withstand the sudden assault of his enemy but he could not stand the sympathy of his friends. Something profoundly shattering was going on in his soul all these days. And yet he did not understand. With the result that eventually he broke out profusely in cursing—yet not God but the day of his birth (3.1). Job began to murmur, to complain, and to question. Why should I have ever seen the light of day in the first place? It is better not to have lived at all! Why should a person live on with so much suffering? Why does God not simply crush me, allow me to die? For there is comfort in death and there is peace in the grave. Why should these many things happen to me? What is the meaning of it all? (3.3ff.)

PLEASE NOTE THAT these sentiments are from the lips of one who had so recently and bravely asserted: Shall we not receive evil from God as we have received good? Should this very same person now turn around and declare: "I would rather die, I do not want to live, it is too much to live"? Is this not highly inconsistent? Why is it that Job, who at the beginning could stand so firmly and so heroicly before the enemy, could *at this moment* capitulate and cave in before his friends? Is it not truly a contradiction? We need to inquire into this matter more fully.

Experience will tell us that in the time of crisis we may call up all our spiritual reserve to meet a trial and seem to overcome it; but afterwards, we begin to assess the situation and as we do so a counter response sets in. Very often in our spiritual experiences, following a great victory even, there will be a setback. And why? Because we have *exhausted our reserves.* The most difficult and trying time is not at the hour of crisis; it is at the time immediately after the crisis. After the critical moment has passed there comes in a reflection, followed then by a reaction. And it was during such a period of reflection and reaction that Job experienced a deep soul searching within himself—and this is represented, I believe, by the encounter and the debates between Job and his three friends which occurred after the crisis had come.

As Job in the silent presence of his "comforters" began to reflect upon his situation he found he could not understand. He was puzzled, confused. Here he was, a man who had been under the care and blessing of God continually; and having over the years prospered immensely as a result, he had accumulated a large family and extensive possessions. He had become great in the eyes of all men. Yet suddenly everything has been yanked away from him; he has been left naked. Although at the moment it happened he immediately afterwards readily acknowledged that he would return naked at life's end and that he must accept bad from God as well as good, he cannot now understand why this calamity should happen to *him*. To him who all his life had feared the Lord and walked before Him in the best way he knew how. To him who had been righteous and perfect in heart. To him who so far as he knew had not sinned against the Lord. Why should God therefore do this to *him?*

Job was cast into utter perplexity. He confessed that he was now "a man whose way is hid, and whom God hath hedged in" (3.23). He could no longer see his way through because God, instead of it being for better, had hedged him in for worse. Yet is this not truly amazing? For this was precisely the opposite to what Satan had accused God of. Satan, we will remember, had accused

Him of hedging in His servant for good; but Job at this moment has misunderstood God's action toward him as being for ill! Unmistakably, a counter response has begun to settle in Job's heart.

Here is shown the agony of a soul who is under the attack of the enemy but also under the discipline of the Lord. For in the final analysis, Job is under the discipline of God, although in outward appearance it would seem he is under the enemy's assault. Unfortunately, however, what is also shown is the ease with which a man in suffering will give way to such a misunderstanding of the Lord. On the one side Job could not deny that God is just and will judge according to man's deeds, that He will see to it that the righteous are rewarded and the wicked are punished. On the other side, though, Job maintained that so far as he knew he was a righteous man. What, then, he reasoned, can be the explanation for this which has befallen me? Why have I been so harshly treated?

In such a dilemma as this, a man might be tempted to adopt an extreme view toward God: either denying that He is just, or that He cares at all in the affairs of men, or that He even exists. But Job could not renounce the Lord in any of these respects, because he knew Him far too well for that. Even though he could not understand, he dared not and would not curse God, for there still remained that restraint in him. So that in spite of his many sufferings and in spite of the unswerving confidence he had in his own integrity, Job just could not bring himself to deny God or His justice. Even though he felt himself righteous, he could not do it. Yet how to reconcile God's justice with his own apparent righteousness left him in total bewilderment. The incomprehensibility of it all produced such extreme grief and anguish within him that as a consequence Job began to curse the day of his birth. Because of his outward sufferings and his inward misery, he began to wish himself dead. Unable to contain himself any longer he commenced, as we saw earlier, to murmur and to complain against God for allowing him to live on and to suffer.

Now for us to term Job's reaction as complaint or murmur is not, I believe, too severe a judgment. And yet, can we at all blame him for this? I hardly think so, for we would do the same, if not even worse. For such an experience as this often happens to us, does it not, when we come into a time of confusion and disturbance and perplexity? We tend to think, as did Job, that it is better for us to die than to live. Yet we, like him, do not know the privilege of existing. We do not realize that God is the God of the living and not the God of the dead. At such a time we so easily forget that there is a meaning to life, and hence we lash out with: Why should I any longer be here? Why does God not take away my life? Why does He allow me to live on? Very simply, dear friends, it is because He has a purpose to fulfill in you and me. His purpose is to mature us.

Yet God's way to spiritual maturity is quite different from our thought. His way and thought are always higher than ours. We think if we trust the Lord we shall flourish, for to us peace and prosperity or wealth represent spiritual favor or maturity. But we do not realize that the transition from childhood and adolescence to manhood is a painful one. We are not prepared for the drastic manner it often seemingly takes when it comes upon us: from relative prosperity to radical poverty, from undisturbed happiness to thorough suffering! How unhappy we feel at being deprived, at being reduced, made naked and poor in the sight of all. Yet this process of transition is so very necessary, because a great deal that is in us is still in the natural. Due to our not seeing sufficiently the difference between the soul and the spirit or not seeing it at all, much yet remains in the soulish realm, and hence the necessity for purification. Many of our so-called spiritual gifts and graces must go down into death. We must lose all that we may gain all—even Christ himself.

Much of this, though, is ofttimes unknown to the soul under chastisement. So that the transition becomes almost unbearable. We are greatly disturbed. Greatly perplexed. We are at a complete loss to understand or to cope with the situation. And as a result, we believe it far better if we do not live on, if we die early—nay, if we had not even been born at all! Why should we come to birth and suffer these things? What is the meaning and purpose of life if *that* is all there is to it? It would be better for us to be non-existent.

And hence, like Job, we turn to cursing ourselves and the day of our birth. Instead of considering God's purpose we become completely involved in ourselves. We become self-centered. This will always be the case when we are only dwelling on our own trouble. We become so absorbed in our problems that we lose sight of God's ultimate purpose. Like Job we would rather die and be done with it so as to gain some immediate comfort for ourselves. How a mighty prince has fallen indeed!

Here then is Job, a soul who was fully exposed, a soul that was stripped naked by God, a soul who entered into a crucible of trials, a soul that was undergoing the process of the deeper working of the cross, but a soul, too, who did not understand what was happening. He dared not renounce God nor the righteousness of God; nonetheless, he could not deny his own righteousness either.

NOW IT WAS as God's servant sat under such a cloud of puzzlement and bewilderment as this that his three friends, once they heard him cursing the day of his birth, began to teach him. They professed to know the way of God, but they were even more ignorant of it than Job. And although they came with good intention, they only ended up adding to his sufferings. They had arrived as the best of friends but they nearly departed as the worst of enemies. For as we shall soon notice, the one principle or truth which in unison these three friends consistently held over Job was just this: God punishes the evil and rewards the good (see for example, 4.7–9, 8.20, 20.4–7). To them this is a truth which is basic, firm, and unchangeable. And as they beheld the sufferings of Job, they could not understand why it was that such an apparently righteous man, such a good man, should suffer so much; and yet, as they attempted to comprehend what they saw, their limited knowledge and understanding forced them to but one conclusion: it *must* be that secretly, Job, you have sinned greatly and this accounts for why you were punished, and punished severely.

Job's friends had come with the purpose of comforting him, but they ended up insisting that God, being just, simply could not be found punishing the good: He will most certainly be found punishing the wicked: and here you are, Job, being punished—and being punished to such degree that it must be because you have committed some secret sin which is most hideous: and though perhaps hidden from man, it is not hidden from God: and because you have done this thing, therefore you are suffering greatly: accordingly, confess your sin to God, Job, and the days of comfort will return; days of refreshing will come from the Lord. This was the only thing they could say because this was the only thing they knew.

LET US ASK ourselves, Is what they said true? Certainly, it is. For if we overthrow this truth, the whole universe will become chaos. Of course God is just! Of course God is the Judge of the whole earth! Of course God punishes the wicked! Of course God rewards the righteous! This is the fundamental underpinning of the moral universe, the principle of sowing and reaping: whatever a person sows, that he reaps. How can we dare overthrow this? If this basic tenet is overturned, then everything will become a nightmare. The three friends of Job tenaciously held on to this one truth, a truth that unquestionably is of great significance.

But, it is not the whole truth. For there may sometimes be in operation other truth than the one. We know, I am sure, that God is greater than any one truth—He is not bound by any one principle. Yes, the Lord works according to principle or truth; but at one time He may use this principle and at another time He may use that principle. We can never be successful in trying to circumscribe our God. He is greater than any law, and in the particular situation with Job God was acting according to a higher law than this fundamental one of sowing and reaping. Yes, this one principle which Job's three friends saw *is* true, universally so. But the application of it has to be accomplished by the Holy Spirit.

In individual cases there can be exceptions, not in the sense of overturning the fundamental truth, but in the sense that there may be other truth in operation. This is something we have to learn. Occasionally we take hold of a spiritual maxim and try to universalize by applying it to everybody. But even though it is true, sometimes the application cannot be generalized. And this is what we find in the instance of Job. In his case God is applying a different principle than that fundamental axiom of the universe which the three friends were emphasizing. God has not overthrown it (as we shall see shortly) but is dealing with His servant at a particular point by the application of a higher principle, even the truth of chastisement, of discipline, of child-training. And this is quite distinct from the other truth.

But at that time, of course, Job and his friends did not know it. And consequently the three "comforters" insisted that Job must have sinned, but the more they insisted the more he rebelled. For he repeatedly and emphatically declared, "I was *not* sinful; I am righteous!" And this is the dilemma into which Job was cast. On the one side he could not overturn this foundational truth; for he recognized and acknowledged that there is a righteousness and a just recompense in the universe; God punishes sin and rewards righteousness. On the other side, however, Job's own experience seemed to contradict this basic axiom. Yet not only his own personal experience seemed to tell him this, but also, as he made closer examination of what actually happens in the world he was forced to the conclusion that the just recompense he readily acknowledged is not always the case (see 21.7ff.). Hence Job deeply felt that what his three friends were pressing upon him to accept just could not be applied to him, although he did not know why. And this is the explanation for all the confusion which eventually arose. We would do well to keep this in mind as we proceed in our consideration of this book.

HAVING THUS DESCRIBED in general terms the mood and direction of the discussion and debates which ensued, let us now take a more detailed look at the three friends and what they and Job had to say. According to the custom of that time, the discussion was carried on in a very orderly manner. None interrupted while the other was speaking. Moreover, there were three cycles of speeches, and within each cycle each friend was given the opportunity to speak once, followed, in every instance, by Job's reply. And as we earlier saw before, it was Job who broke the awful seven days' silence by opening up the discussion with bemoaning the day of his birth. So that immediately afterward, Eliphaz, the first of the three friends, launched the initial round of debate between himself and Job (Chapters 4–7).

Eliphaz to me represents outwardly mysticism and inwardly, the emotion of the soul. Being the chief spokesman and leader of the group (cf. 42.7b), Eliphaz now stepped forth to lay down the main line of argument. His intention was to instruct Job. Yet all his instructions were based upon some mystical experience. Very early in his speech Eliphaz had this to say, which is quite revealing:

> *Now a thing was secretly brought to me,*
> *And mine ear received a whisper thereof.*
> *In thoughts from the visions of the night,*
> *When deep sleep falleth on men,*
> *Fear came upon me, and trembling,*
> *Which made all my bones to shake.*
> *Then a spirit passed before my face;*
> *The hair of my flesh stood up.*
> *It stood still, but I could not discern the*
> *appearance thereof;*

> *A form was before mine eyes:*
> *There was silence, and I heard a voice, saying,*
>   *Shall mortal man be more just than God?*
> *Shall a man be more pure than his Maker?*
>   *Behold, he putteth no trust in his servants;*
> *And his angels he chargeth with folly:*
>   *How much more them that dwell in houses of clay,*
> *Whose foundation is in the dust,*
>   *Who are crushed like the moth!* (4.12–19)

Eliphaz based all his instruction upon secret experience. Said he, A spirit appeared to me: my hair stood up: I was frightened; then I heard a voice declare: Shall a mortal man be more just than God? Shall a man be purer than his Maker? Certainly then, concluded Eliphaz to Job, it must be that you have sinned. Quite extraordinary is it not? The whole experience of this friend was founded upon mysticism, upon something strange and mysterious: a spirit appeared to him.

IN A VERY broad sense, dear friends, every Christian is a mystic; because by that term is simply meant, one who seeks the Lord with his heart, one who seeks an inner experience of God. So that in a very general way every Christian is a mystic, since we have to know God inwardly; otherwise we do not know Him at all. But mysticism as a body of teaching and practice is something else. In this respect mysticism is not something restricted just to Christianity. On the contrary, in this regard it has its adherents not only in the Christian world but also among many people who are unbelievers.

Perhaps a few words on the subject will not be out of place here and may be of some help to us all. For we should try to acquaint ourselves with a number of the more important features which are generally common to all such adherents of mysticism. What follows is but a few of them. First of all, mystics believe that within each person there is a spark of divine life, and that all a person needs to know is how to bring out that spark. This is not at all scriptural. For in and of ourselves, none of us has that life. Divine life is only to be found in Christ. It is only when we believe in the Lord Jesus that we receive this life. And hence, to begin with, the mystic starts from an altogether erroneous proposition.

But secondly, mystics in some sense trust in the merits of their own sufferings. They believe there is virtue in suffering, which is to say that they cannot get away from a feeling of doing penance, which idea is wrong. For we know that we overcome, not because of how much *we* suffer, but because of the sufferings of *Christ.*

And thirdly, the mystic does not see the difference between the soul and the spirit. For him it is a mixed experience. Very often we will find in the writings of the mystic features that are no doubt highly spiritual; nevertheless, these spiritual things are mixed in deeply with those that are highly soulical.

And finally, mystics have a tendency to fall into emotionalism. They mistake emotional experience for *spiritual* experience. We do not know who that spirit was that appeared to Eliphaz. He spoke of a spirit speaking to him, but he mentioned how he had been put in fear by it. I wonder if this is the right spirit; I doubt it is the Holy Spirit. Though it seems to voice the truth, it is more a projection of the spirit of Eliphaz than an appearing of the Holy Spirit. Yes, in any given instance, a right word may be spoken, but it may not necessarily be a right spirit that accompanies it. Oh, the testing and proving of the spirit is something God wants us to do. It is not true that every spirit is good. There are good spirits and there are bad spirits, and we are obligated—nay, even commanded—to test each one (1 John 4.1).

WE MAY SAY, therefore, that outwardly Eliphaz represents mysticism. When a person is confronted with a spiritual crisis mysticism attempts to explain it. And as the mystic sees it, all suffering is due to sin, and yet there is more to such suffering than mere punishment. The mystic tries without success to resolve the dilemma in the crisis by saying that there is merit in suffering for sin, that the suffering which flows out from the punishment is itself a purification.

Occasionally you do find something commendable in mysticism; for example, Eliphaz mentioned the matter of correction: "Behold, happy is the man whom God correcteth: therefore despise not thou the chastening of the Almighty" (5.17). God may be correcting you, he says to Job. Eliphaz did in fact allow for the possibility of correction in God's dealing, yet his understanding of chastisement was more on the negative side of punishment than on the positive side of conforming unto maturity—that is, child-training, son-forming. The sense of *positive* correction is very slight in Eliphaz. His primary instruction to Job was that which was commonly accepted: the evil are punished while the good are rewarded. He did not at first charge directly that Job had sinned and therefore he suffered; however, he did imply that this must be the case.

BUT WE MAY also view Eliphaz as, inwardly, the emotion of the soul. In this sense a person becomes involved in his feelings. How they are worked up whenever we are thrown into a situation we do not understand. In that hour they will begin to stir and highly involve us emotionally in the situation. And because we are God-fearing persons, our feelings will tell us that God must be just. So our emotions, as represented here by Eliphaz, at first make an attempt to justify God: Can a mortal man be more righteous than He? Impossible! The Lord is just, we say, and can do no wrong. There must therefore be a reason for such suffering. And so, we judge, it must be because there is sin, terrible sin. How our feelings do take on the appearance of standing for God and with God.

In countering this jab of Eliphaz', Job's answer reveals equally the emotional reaction. For he declared that he had been terrified in dreams and visions. Yes,

Eliphaz, you say you have had a mystical experience which revealed, Can a man be more just than God? Yet I too have had such dreams and visions; but I was nearly crushed.

Dear friends, we are aware, are we not, of how frightening such an experience as this can be? One feeling declares, God is just. Another one counters with, True, I cannot deny that God is a just Judge, rewarding the good and punishing the wicked; yet I have to maintain that I am righteous nonetheless. How feeling fights back and forth within Job. One emotion says, God is righteous; the other replies, But I too am righteous. One speaks of visions and dreams which justify God; the other speaks of visions and dreams which terrify and crush him. Job was on the verge of breaking down. Unable to stand it any longer, he had to let loose his pent-up feeling. Because he was in such bitterness of heart, Job had to ask that he would not be reproved for his words (see 7.11, 6.24f.). Why did God make him a target and why did He not forgive his transgression (7.20,21)?

How changeable is our emotional life. One moment we feel this way and the next moment the other. Yet how can we reconcile these two contrary feelings and see through to God? With emotion it is impossible. We have to rise above our feeling if we would see Him.

THUS ENDS THE first round of debate between Job and

Eliphaz. In the second round, recorded in Chapters 15–17, each of them still maintained the same position, for emotionally none can rise above what he is: emotion represents the person, it does not represent God. Eliphaz accused Job, saying, "Yea, thou makest piety of none effect . . . for thy mouth uttereth thine iniquity" (15.4a, 5a Darby). Moreover, he restated his original thesis in this way:

> *What is a man, that he should be clean?*
>   *And he that is born of a woman, that he should*
>   *be righteous?*
> *Behold, he putteth no trust in his holy ones;*
>   *Yea, the heavens are not clean in his sight:*
> *How much less one that is abominable and corrupt,*
>   *A man that drinketh iniquity like water!* (*15.14–16*)

Eliphaz still took the mystical approach. He cited how the unrighteous were always punished.

In reply, Job told Eliphaz that he was a "miserable comforter"; that he did not know what he was talking about, for he was not in the same position as he, Job, was (16.2–4). He lamented again his many woes. How God had crushed him! Yet he still had faith that there was a witness in heaven for him (16.19). And then he asked for an arbitrator: "Mine eye poureth out tears unto God, that one might plead for a man with God, as a son of man pleadeth for his neighbor!" (16.20b,21 mg.) But when none was forthcoming he was plunged again into hopelessness. Emotion proves to be very volatile and fickle. When it is not satisfied, it will grope in darkness and experience many moments of ups and downs. Unquestionably it demonstrates the lack of any kind of stability.

❧

THE THIRD ROUND of debates between these two is found in Chapters 22 to 24. Eliphaz opened up immediately with a question. "Can a man be profitable unto God? Surely he that is wise is profitable unto himself" (22.2). Once again, what Eliphaz says is partly true, but it is not the whole truth; for we *can* be profitable to God in that we may serve His purpose and manifest His glory.

We next find that Eliphaz—seeing he could not subdue him through the emotional appeal of saying: You had better repent, Job, and then God will be good to you—ultimately becomes angry and commences to accuse. Instead of appreciating the dilemma of Job and his bitterness of soul, he now makes strong accusation against him. Chapter 22 is a terribly unjust indictment of God's servant. When Eliphaz cannot reason with him, he begins in that chapter to bring many grave charges against him; but these are plainly false accusations, because in the latter chapter, 24, Job takes the exact opposite position on the very matters of which he has been accused. Nevertheless Eliphaz believed them to be true, yet not because he had any proof but because he was so emotionally involved with his own thesis.

In his response, found in Chapter 23, Job expressed the confidence that God would not refuse to argue with him (vv.3–7). The trouble was, though, that he could not find God (vv.3,8–9). He ended up agreeing with Eliphaz that the wicked would eventually be punished.

Is not all this just like emotion? Our feeling is so unsettled, shifting its position continually. At one moment we defend God. At another moment we defend ourselves. At one time we try to make appeals, at another time we grow angry, even sometimes indulging in false self-accusations. Our soul has become thoroughly aroused emotionally, so aroused in fact, that it well-nigh reaches the point of a nervous breakdown. Several times, as a matter of fact, Job himself nearly collapsed.

THIS CONFRONTATION of Eliphaz with Job highlights so clearly the stirring of the feelings within the human soul during a critical trial. Look into your own experience and see if this is not true. Whenever you run up against some extremely difficult situation the emotion will invariably be the first element to be stirred up within you. Yet it is incapable of solving the problem, since it alternates between one position and another. It can be very unreasonable. In fact, the emotions are not rational in the least. And having gone through such a searching in the emotion of your soul, you come out with the distinct awareness that nothing in the slightest has been accomplished.

Even though, in Job's case, there were these three rounds of discussion and debate, nothing at all was answered, nothing at all was gained. Emotion as it were does not help in penetrating the mind of God nor can it explain the mysterious way of God. Mysticism may give us many beautiful and worthy thoughts, but it cannot bring us closer to God. We need a revelation of the Lord himself. Until it is calmed by the revelation of God, emotion will not be stilled and delivered from self. For it is like the tumultuous sea which tosses a ship so violently about. Our Lord himself is needed to calm the sea of our feelings and to bring our ship to harbor. We like Job can be so emotionally involved with our problem that we are well-nigh sunk in it. But when we see God, we shall be able to rise above such an involvement and thus be delivered from it. The way of maturity, it becomes evident, lies far deeper than the path of emotion.

THE SECOND FRIEND who tried to comfort Job, yet ended up condemning him, was Bildad. Bildad, I believe, outwardly represents traditionalism and inwardly, the mind of the soul. Bildad on the one hand represents the person who takes the traditional view of things. He on the other hand represents the mind that searches into the past.

This is made plain from an early passage in Bildad's first round of debate with Job (Chapters 8–10). In that passage he is found confidently asserting these words:

> *Inquire, I pray thee, of the former age,*
> *And apply thyself to that which their fathers*
> *have searched out:*

(For we are but of yesterday, and know nothing,
Because our days upon earth are a shadow:)
Shall not they teach thee, and tell thee,
And utter words out of their heart? (8.8–10)

Bildad, unlike Eliphaz, did not base his instruction upon mystic experiences; he instead founded his teaching upon the tradition of the fathers. True, he took the same stance as did Eliphaz, maintaining like Job's first friend: "Doth God pervert justice? or doth the Almighty pervert righteousness?" (8.3) But he in addition reached back to the past and tried to establish his argument by means of tradition. We in our day know nothing, says Bildad, but our fathers—oh, they have made intense researches into these matters, and surely their conclusion cannot be wrong! And what was their conclusion? God will never pervert His judgment: the wicked shall be punished and the good shall be rewarded: and if there is suffering, there must be sin: the wicked cannot stand (8.11–22). And Bildad, seeing nothing else, held fast to this one axiom of the ancients. He argued from the tradition of the fathers.

LET US PAUSE for a moment and consider this matter of tradition, because sometimes we can go to extremes on the subject. Some people advocate the complete discarding of all tradition, whereas others hold tenaciously to every bit of it. Now tradition is not altogether bad. It is merely the accumulation of past knowledge and experience. It is, however, a great mixture. On the one side it has this advantage, that it does stabilize society. If there is no tradition society will fall apart. But on the other side it also has a disadvantage, in that it hinders progress. It is continually harking back to the old, to the past—and the older the better. With the result that tradition becomes fixed and inflexible. There being nothing new in it, any kind of progress is automatically retarded, if not ruled out altogether. So that tradition can be very strengthening, but it can be a bondage too.

We need to see that we should not cast away *all* tradition. For believers, there are Christian traditions which simply must be kept. They are their heritage. And this is the very term used by Paul. In 1 Corinthians 11.2 the apostle wrote these words: "Now I praise you that ye remember me in all things, and hold fast the traditions, even as I delivered them to you." Here Paul commended the believers in Corinth because they had been keeping the traditions or the instructions he had given them. Paul expresses the same thought and uses the same word in his second letter to the saints at Thessalonica: "So then, brethren, stand fast, and hold the traditions which ye were taught, whether by word, or by epistle of ours" (2.15; see also 3.6).

Believers need to recognize the fact that in the Christian faith there are traditions coming from the Lord and handed down to them by the early apostles which they must keep. For instance, the Lord's table. Not too long ago I happened to be among a certain group of believers. These saints were quite free in the

Lord; and because they desired so greatly to be free of every and all bondage, this issue of the breaking of bread arose as a real problem. Each Sunday they would have the Lord's table prepared but placed off in a corner somewhere. And why? Because they never knew whether they would actually break the bread that day or not. If the Spirit should so lead, they would break the bread. But if not, they would merely leave it in the corner unbroken. Now the reason for this was that some of the saints thought they should not observe tradition; therefore, they argued, we should or should not have the Lord's table every Sunday only as the Spirit leads. Is that being spiritual? I hardly think so. For the breaking of bread on the Lord's Day is but one of in fact several traditions we Christians must keep.

Paul said for us to hold fast to tradition. And tradition if it originates with God is not something bad. It in that respect comprises those matters which have come down from God through the apostles, and these are items we have to observe. But of course it is most important that we observe them in spirit, not merely in form.

Yet there is such a thing as the traditions of the fathers; such traditions tend to obscure the Spirit of God; and from these we must indeed be freed. For it was the "tradition of the fathers" that our Lord Jesus himself vehemently opposed. He inveighed against it in His day because those who kept the tradition of the fathers did so to such an extent that they broke the law of God (see Matt. 15.3,6; cf. Mark 7.13). And to do that becomes a bondage. Dear brethren, never be bound by the tradition of the fathers but recognize that you and I have an obligation to hold fast the tradition delivered to us by God.

So here came Bildad to Job, grounding all his teachings upon tradition; yet this tradition which he leaned upon was not the full counsel of God but was the tradition of the ancients. It tended to bondage instead of liberation; for it was but half the truth, not the whole. And that was what Bildad represented outwardly.

⚜

BUT THIS SECOND FRIEND also represents in an inward way the work of the mind. This working of the mind is disclosed in 8.11 where Bildad is observed to wonder: "Can the papyrus grow up without mire? Can the reed-grass grow without water?" (mg.) To Bildad there is a cause and an effect in everything, and none can change it. What is this but the operation of the mind?

Now our mind is supposed to be logical, rational. It reasons and connects the effect with the cause. But it can also be deductive as well as inductive. It can draw conclusions out of the past data. In spite of its ability, however, we have to acknowledge that our mind is darkened, that our own light is very darkness itself. Man can never, by searching, find out God. How our mind, even the best of our reasoning, obscures the will of God. And this that is before us is a typical case, wherein, as we shall see, neither tradition nor the human mind can solve the spiritual problem.

In answer Job said: "Of a truth I know that it is so: but how can man be just with God?" (9.1) This statement shows that Job's mind was really puzzled. It was active and probing. He acknowledged that God is wise and powerful, that man is no match for Him; He can do anything, and who can resist? In his answer Job showed great knowledge. In confessing the power of God, he noted that God is free to do whatever He likes and He does just that (9.3–12). Moreover, none is perfect before Him, and hence there is no difference: the righteous perish as well as the wicked: "It is all one; therefore I say, he destroyeth the perfect and the wicked" (9.22). Job here has searched his own mind but could not understand why God should oppress the one whom He himself has made (10.2–3).

⚜

IN THE SECOND round (Chapters 18–19) Bildad has absolutely nothing new to offer. For tradition is based upon the old, the past. A person who likes the old wine is prejudiced against anything new. Like tradition, he will not even consider the possibility of fresh ideas. Tradition simply ignores the new and insists on the old. Accordingly, Bildad merely renews his statement of how the wicked are punished by God. His mind seemed all the more to be in bondage to the past.

Job, on the other hand, manifested a mental faculty which was free from tradition. His was an open and acute mind, a mind that did not consider itself under any obligation toward such tradition, because he judged that there were instances—and especially in his own case—where the teaching of the ancients just did not apply. From his reply to Bildad in this second round we can see that Job was not bound in the slightest by the past. Nevertheless, though his thought was free, though it possessed great knowledge, neither could *he* penetrate the mystery of life.

Job agreed with Bildad that it was God who had overthrown him, but he argued that his friends ought not persecute him as God had; instead they should have pity on him (see 19.6 mg. and 19.21–22). How fitting this request is. How we need to learn this lesson in sensitivity. Whenever the Lord judges, do we dare judge also? It is the will of God that we should be merciful that we ourselves may obtain mercy (Matt. 5.7; cf. 2 Sam. 22.26).

Job could not fathom why God's hand should be upon him; yet out of desperation he seemed at one point to rise up in faith:

> *As for me I know that my Redeemer liveth,*
> *And at last he will stand up upon the earth:*
> *And after my skin, even this body, is destroyed,*
> *Then without my flesh shall I see God;*
> *Whom I, even I, shall see for myself,*
> *And mine eyes shall behold, and not as a*
> *stranger.* (*19.25–27 mg.*)

Faith rises above the reasoning of the mind. What our thought cannot explain and penetrate, faith enters into. How blessed it is to know that my Redeemer lives! He is my kinsman-redeemer. He is the "goel" who will avenge and vindicate me. (For this word in the Hebrew text signifies the closest kinsman by whom a person may be avenged for some wrong.) My Redeemer lives, affirms Job, therefore I can trust in Him. He shall stand up upon the earth at the last day, for He shall come to the earth and judge. It may not happen in my lifetime, nevertheless there is resurrection; and in resurrection I shall yet see Him with my own eyes. What penetrating faith was displayed in Job.

CHAPTERS 25 and 26 record the third but extremely short round of debates between the two. And this quite probably is because Bildad again has nothing new to offer. He merely reiterates the already overworked statement that God is all-powerful and none is pure before Him (25.2–4). Job once more agrees with Bildad that God is almighty, for has He not hanged the earth on nothing? And who can understand the thunder of His power? (26.7,14b) He can only conclude by admitting: "Lo, these are but the outskirts of his ways: and how small a whisper do we hear of him!" (26.14a) What the mind of the present as well as the past has searched out, acknowledges Job ruefully, are but the outskirts, the borders, of God's ways. Man has not yet penetrated into the center of His thought. For even with this border knowledge, he fails to hear God's speech. Man barely hears His whisper even.

How TOTALLY INADEQUATE is our mind in the things of God. When confronted by some critical circumstance our mind, like Job's, begins to search and to search and to search diligently for an answer. But whether it is the mind represented by Bildad or the mind represented by Job, whether it is our thought influenced by the tradition of the fathers or our thought that is free to move, we learn inescapably that neither way can yield the right answer to our difficulty.

Do not think because you have a mind which is free from tradition that you will therefore find a solution. You will not. Our mind is darkened, its light is itself darkness. It is only as we are in God's light that we can see light (Ps. 36.9). No matter how much we search, we will not find God. That will only confuse us. Let us humbly accept the verdict that the mind simply does not help.

Zophar is the last of Job's three "comforters". He was probably the oldest among them all, and certainly the most impatient of all. His first round with Job can be read in Chapters 11 to 14. His words were blunt and his accusation was direct. We may therefore say that outwardly Zophar represents dogmatism and inwardly, the will of the soul. He did not draw his inspiration from spirit or dream, neither did he rely on tradition. He merely gave his opinion in an absolute way. Zophar simply tried to overwhelm Job with the sense of: What do *you* know?—

> *Canst thou by searching find out God?*
> *Canst thou find out the Almighty unto perfection?*
> *It is high as heaven; what canst thou do?*
> *Deeper than Sheol; what canst thou know?* (11.7–8)

Whereupon Zophar in dogmatic fashion exhorted him to repent; and then, said he, days of comfort will come to you, Job, once again (11.13–19).

⚜

LET US RECOGNIZE that there is a difference between dogma and doctrine. Sometimes we should be a little bit careful with the use of words. Do we not at times hear ourselves say, "We don't want any doctrine!" But as a matter of simple fact, we *have* to have it. If we have no doctrine we have no truth, and we therefore have no basis for spiritual experience.

Doctrine is teaching. Doctrine is truth. The doctrine of the New Testament is the basis of our faith. How then can we do without it? We cannot. Clearly, there *is* a place for foundation truth. Yet it is something which ought to come from God and not from man. If it derives from God it places a spiritual obligation upon us; but if it derives from man it becomes a bondage.

97

Admittedly, doctrine alone is not enough. There must be experience following the doctrine. But no one can say he does not want doctrine. If anyone does not want this he does not have true experience. For doctrine is related to faith, and faith is related to will, and will is related to experience. Hence everything is based upon doctrine, upon truth.

Dogma, however, is a different matter. Perhaps a definition of dogma and dogmatism can help us here. Dogma, says Webster, frequently suggests an arrogant insistence upon authority; and, says Webster again, dogmatism denotes a positiveness in assertion in matters of opinion—the stating of a view or belief in such a manner as though it were an established fact. Dogma, we may therefore say, is a certain teaching arrogantly asserted with a force of authority as though it were an established fact. That is a dogma. True, we have to accept certain doctrines of God, but we should never be dogmatic. By all means there is authority in doctrine or truth, but to be dogmatic in its pronouncement constitutes an attempt to exert authority by ourselves. Certainly we should know the truth, and as the Lord Jesus said, in knowing the truth the truth shall set us free (John 8.32). If the truth or doctrine is of God it will emancipate us instead of putting us in bondage.

But let us note as well that the application of truth is something which must be left flexible. It should not, as is the case with dogma, be applied indiscriminately. Truth must only be used as the Spirit leads. If left in the hands of the Holy Spirit, truth will be flexibly applied and will ultimately liberate. But dogma is in the hands of man or of a human institution, and is more often than not applied without any discrimination. As such, dogma becomes something fixed and inflexible and will oppress rather than release.

THUS WE HAVE Zophar coming to Job with his dogma. And what was his approach? The reader will find that he made sweeping statements, which were truths in theory but were not the whole truth. As they applied to God's servant, these "memorable sayings" of Zophar's were in Job's view nothing but "proverbs of ashes" (13.12). His dogmas were so absolute as to leave no room for any latitude. His judgments were therefore harsh. What Zophar had done was to oversimplify truth. Yes, truth is absolute and simple and clear; nevertheless, its application and explanation must be in the Spirit, thus affording it a certain degree of flexibility. But in the wrong hands it can be oversimplified and thus become dogmatic. And dogmatism never helps to solve spiritual problems; it only overpowers and suppresses. It brings people into bondage, never into freedom.

With an attitude such as this, then, Zophar quite naturally pronounces the central dogma of all: God rewards the good but He punishes the wicked (20.4ff.); therefore, Job, you *must* have sinned, since you are under such severe punishment.

Let us observe, though, that in making his response to Zophar Job manifested equally as strong a will as his friend did. Not only did he deny that he had sinned—continuing to maintain before all his righteous integrity—but he also rejected every other dogma of Zophar's. He professed that he knew as much, if not more, than his friend (12.2–3). Job contended that God does things according to *His* wish, and that He brings counsellors, kings, priests, and elders to nought (v.17ff.). "With him is strength and wisdom; the deceived and the deceiver are his" (12.16). He refuted Zophar's saying that God was unsearchable, for he insisted: "I will speak to the Almighty, and will find pleasure in reasoning with God" (13.3 Darby).

Once again, out of desperation Job declared his faith in God: "Behold, if he slay me, yet would I trust in him; but I will defend mine own ways before him" (13.15 Darby). Such faith he emphatically affirmed, even though he could not understand why God should desire to slay him. He wondered why He did not forgive and let him alone. Job was far more flexible than Zophar, and certainly he was not dogmatic. Yet as can be seen from the latter part of verse 15, it was still in the realm of the will: "Nevertheless I will argue my ways before him" (ASV mg.).

❧

NOTHING NEW is presented for consideration in the second round (Chapters 20 and 21). Zophar held to the same dogma as before but this time couched it in a threatening way. He was completely out of touch with reality and fact and utterly lacking in human sympathy. Here he was, a person seemingly zealous for God, and yet he completely misrepresented Him, for he had no heart for the weak and the feeble. Job on the other hand tried to present actual facts that he plainly witnessed in the world about him, although at the same time he could not totally reject the truth; which left him quite puzzled and frequently made him incoherent in his speech.

There is no third round. And why? Because the one who is dogmatic will give up on others very quickly. You either conform or you are given up by the dogmatist as hopeless.

Do take note from these rounds of debate between Zophar and Job that the more anyone tries by dogma to force a person the more that person will resist and rebel. It turns entirely into a test of wills: the will of Zophar versus the will of Job. And both have iron wills; none will yield to the other. Such a confrontation between these two simply illustrates the two sides of Job's will, and of our wills too. Often you and I will say, "Will, let me believe." Yet that will of ours rebels. It instead counters with, "I cannot, for I am righteous; I simply cannot believe." This is a conflict of the will within the person.

BEFORE US, THEREFORE, is a soul wracked by a deep spiritual crisis, in which neither mysticism nor traditionalism nor dogmatism can ever help. Admittedly, there are values in mysticism; but of course there are many errors too. If one reads the sayings of Eliphaz he will find, on the positive side, many precious thoughts. For instance Eliphaz suggested to Job,

> *Lay thou thy treasure in the dust,*
>   *And the gold of Ophir among the stones of the*
>   *brooks;*
> *And the Almighty will be thy treasure,*
>   *And precious silver unto thee.*
> *For then shalt thou delight thyself in the Almighty,*
>   *And shalt lift up thy face unto God.* (22.24–26)

If you put away your gold and silver, Job, and really love God with your whole heart, you will find He is more precious than anything else. Very good words, these. Nonetheless, despite the salutary thoughts in mysticism, it could not provide the answer to Job's crisis.

Good features are to be found in tradition too. We mentioned before that we should not be bound by the tradition of the fathers but certainly we should keep the tradition of the Lord, those Christian obligations which come from Him and are communicated to us by the early apostles. These are the traditions we should treasure. But though there be a good side to tradition, it likewise does not yield the answer to any spiritual problem.

Doctrine also is something the Christian cannot do without. The Lord Jesus once declared that if a person really desired to do His will, he would know whether

His doctrine or teaching were of God or purely from himself as a man (John 7.17). That person would discover that His doctrine was divine. Doctrine is essential. But to be dogmatic in its pronouncement is something human. It does not, and cannot, convince or convict.

IN SUMMARY, THEN, none of these three approaches can assist in any spiritual trial. Yet in any such trial there will invariably be a soul searching. A person cannot go through a crisis and his soul remain at rest. It is nearly impossible. When you are plunged into any deep waters, your soul, doing its best to locate a solution, will become thoroughly agitated: the emotion will be stirred up, the mind will be activated, and the will will be clashing. Every department of your being is being searched out.

And in one respect you will come to realize that none of these searchings of the soul can provide any satisfactory answer. Struggle and strive as you may, it comes to no positive result. As in the case with Job, you end up precisely where you began, with the spiritual crisis still present; which is what this entire part of JOB manifestly shows: beginning at Chapter 3 and ending at Chapter 31, the reader cannot escape the obvious conclusion that there is no difference: Job, sad to say, has only turned full circle.

In quite another respect, though, can anyone say

that the process is entirely a waste? I do not think so, because as a person is brought to the end of himself in such searching he intermittently discerns flashes of divine light. How interesting in reading through these chapters from 3 to 31 to discover that quite a few streaks of light have come upon that searching soul. When at one point, for instance, Job had in himself no more argument left to put forward to his friends—they just not believing in his innocency, and his inability to prove it to them—he cries out: "Behold, my witness is in heaven, and he that voucheth for me is on high" (16.19). That is his only hope. Or take as another example that flash of faith which shines brilliantly into Job's darkened soul: "I know that my Redeemer liveth, and at last he will stand up upon the earth: and . . . I shall see God" (19.25,26). This is *real* faith. And at still another moment, when Job tries to defend himself he blurts out with: "Though he slay me, yet will I trust in him" (13.15 AV). What a jewel of light *that* is!

The reader cannot help but be struck by these and other shafts of divine illumination which now and again invade that darkened soul; but unfortunately these flashes arise and then as quickly fade away; they do not stay. They are overwhelmed by further agitation of the soul. So far as the soul's searching of itself is concerned, there is really nothing there, nothing in it which will bring the crisis to an end. And so the deep searching continues on until it terminates with what is found in Chapter 31, the contents of which, from one point of view, do not present a very pretty picture. We need to take a deeper look into that chapter.

❧

WE WILL RECALL that in Chapter 29 Job had summed up his life at some length, relating how throughout the past he had been preserved by God and describing what a life he had consequently enjoyed. It had been a life of fellowship with God, a life marked by so much light, a life very full of righteous acts. But in Chapter 30 the reverse has become true. How opposite today from what he had been before. Whereas previously he had been highly esteemed, Job today has become the object of scorn and derision by all—especially by the young and the outcast. Possessed of so much before, he today has been stripped of everything. The cross has worked deeply in his soul. Iron, it seems, has entered into it.

And as Job looked back to bygone days and tried to compare the past with what was now, do you know what ultimately happened? In all his searching of the soul he had become so totally engrossed in himself that by the time of Chapter 31 he has sunk to the only possible state a man in his condition could fall into—a massive indulgence in self-pity, self-righteousness, self-vindication.

Logically, this is all which *can* result, because self- or soul-analysis can only bring us further *into* the soul; it by no means can deliver us *out* of the soul. And this state of affairs is so obviously borne out in Chapter 31, where Job is found winding up his lengthy defense before all three friends at once. For please note that in this chapter he uses the singular personal pronouns of I, my, me, and mine more than 80 times. He is exclusively occupied with himself alone: I, my, mine; and what a *good* I he is at that. He announces in various ways that he is right. He proclaims his attitudes toward sin—how he had never before harbored any secret sin of idolatry —how he had made a covenant with his eyes that he might not sin against God. He declares how he did not love the world, for even though God had given him great wealth he never made gold his hope. He makes known how in the past he had been good to everybody— how he had supplied the wants of all who were needy—how he had been kind even to his enemies—how he had never rejoiced at the destruction of his foes—how he had treated well his servants and maids—etc. etc. etc.

In revealing his glorious past life and in examining his present horrible condition, Job sums it all up with one grand petition to the Lord: "Look here, God, I am such a perfect soul. So far as I know I have never done anything wrong. I am righteous. Here then is my petition: I attach my name to it; now You answer me, God. Answer me: Why is it that for such a man as I, You have treated me so badly? Why is it that *I* should suffer so? Here is my signature. Answer me!" (31.35ff.) And in Chapter 30 he even accuses God of cruelty, declaring, "Once You were kind but now You have become cruel to me. Why do You do that?" (cf. vv.21–22)

Brethren, we never know what is at the bottom of our soul until that day when its depths are measured. In spite of Job's expression, made at the very beginning, of disinterested love toward God, hidden away in that love of his there is that self-willing. True, it is quite accurate to say that Job did not serve God for gain; nevertheless, deep within, he was not ready for loss. Yes, he still trusted in God; yes, he had not denied God; even so, he misunderstood Him. What had happened was that he had been fainting under the chastening hand of the Lord, with the result that his *self* life at its *depths* had been discovered and uncovered. And it all at last came out in a torrent of self-vindication: "I the righteous one, I the right self, will hold on to my righteousness—even before God I will hold on to my integrity. I have not sinned. Why is it that I be punished then? I cannot understand it. It is not fair!" Job dared to challenge God with his own righteousness (cf. 27.5,6).

DEAR FRIENDS, may there not be a lesson in this for us today? Sometimes we think we love God with a disinterested love, and no doubt it is so; but as we are being measured to the very bottom we shall recognize that there is still much mixture in it. Far down in our soul there remains a love of self, there is yet the element of self-pity, of self-righteousness, of self-vindication. What is lacking is that total abandonment to God. If we are entirely abandoned to Him we will not question His will. We will not try to vindicate ourselves. We will instead yield ourselves humbly into His hands and wait for *His* vindication.

But Job, like so many of us, had not arrived at that point yet. It was necessary for the cross to uncover the subtlety of that self of his. The cross has had to break him completely in order that the spirit might be brought forth; and this, as we shall observe in the next Part, is what has happened by the time these tortuous debates between Job and his three friends have been concluded. The process of soul-searching is coming to an end.

PLEASE REALIZE, however, that this process has been necessary to effect the final deliverance. As you go through a spiritual crisis, inevitably there will be these searchings in your soul. Yet it is not altogether unprofitable; for it reveals to you, as nothing else could, the utter incompetency of the soul to resolve any spiritual problem. After such a long period of searching it has arrived at nothing. You finally must admit that your feelings can never lead you out of the crisis, your thoughts can never search out the mind of God, and your will and desiring are not able to bow and to bend under the hand of the Lord. Far from resolving your trial such soul-searchings have actually aggravated it. Such an experience makes very obvious the fact that if ever there is to be a solution that solution will have to come, not from you but from somewhere else. The searching of the soul just does not have the answer.

Our God and our Father, we do acknowledge that our soul can never solve our spiritual problem. Even so, we desire to know our soul as it stands naked before You. We desire to see that in us, that is, in our flesh, there is no good. It is totally incompetent to bring in the answer. We desire to see that our hope is purely in You. O Lord, if there should be anyone going through a period of soul-searching, we pray You will bring him or her out of THAT into Your marvelous light which alone can solve all our difficulties and bring us to Your desired end. Lord, we ask You to use these words, if possible, to help us along our way of following You so that we may not be discouraged nor plunge into despair but that we may press on toward the goal. We pray we may be a people to the praise of Your glory and grace, because we have been redeemed for this very purpose. Be gracious to us and be with us throughout all our days. We ask in the Name of our Lord Jesus. Amen.

PART THREE

The Spirit's Interpretation

I am young, and ye are very old;
   Wherefore I held back, and durst not show you
   mine opinion.
But there is a spirit in man,
   And the breath of the Almighty giveth him
   understanding.
Therefore I said, Hearken to me.

   If there be with him a messenger,
An interpreter, one among a thousand,
   To show unto man what is right for him;
Then God is gracious unto him, and saith,
   Deliver him from going down to the pit,
I have found a ransom.

—ELIHU THE SON OF BARACHEL THE BUZITE

The Spirit's Interpretation

"THE WORDS of Job are ended." What a blessed relief the narrator provides at the conclusion of Chapter 31! *Finally* Job has spoken his last word. Oh, when one comes to that point in the story he can begin to breathe again! At times the reader may have thought that Job's words would never cease. How he seems to be able to go on and on and on, never running out of something to say (yet is that not how we also are?). But thank God, the words of Job were ended.

Yet thank God, too, that this was not *the end.* Just suppose this were actually the closing of the narrative: suppose Job's life had ended before the end of the Lord had been reached: then what a falling short of the purpose of God. But thank God the words of Job *were* ended so that the Lord might begin. And His beginning is found in Chapters 32 to 37 with the words of Elihu.

⚜

IT IS QUITE possible that as Job and his three friends were debating among themselves a large group of people began to gather around. And from among the crowds who were listening stepped forward a young man by the name of Elihu. We do not know this man very well. It is not certain whether he was acquainted with Job and his companions before this event or not. But we do know that Job and his three friends were older individuals, whereas Elihu was a young man. He had been listening in to the conversation of the others. But when the words of Job were finished and the three friends thereafter fell silent, Elihu was greatly stirred in his spirit.

Now the name Elihu means "whose God is He". God is his God. So what does this young man Elihu represent? To me I feel that this man represents the human spirit. When God created man He created him not only with a body and with a soul but also with a spirit.

WE ARE TOLD in John 4 that "God is spirit; and they that worship him must worship in spirit and in truth" (v.24 mg.). And who can worship Him in spirit? Only those who are created with a spirit. Hence all men were created with such a component. Our human spirit is an organ within us for apprehending God. It is by this element within that we can worship God the Spirit. God is not to be apprehended in the body of man, neither in his soul, but He is to be apprehended by man's spirit. But unfortunately because of sins and transgressions our spirit fell dead (though was not annihilated). And consequently, most people do not realize they have a spirit. All they know of is a soul and a body.

I can never forget a lady missionary who led my father to the Lord and who subsequently in her later years stayed with us. She came from Virginia, and every time when something unusual would happen she would throw up her hands and exclaim, Oh my soul and body! Each time she would come out with these words. But she never mentioned the spirit. Now of course she knew about the human spirit. Nevertheless, we do often hear this common expression used among people. Most persons only know of soul and body. They do not in addition know that they have a spirit. Praise God, though, that "that which is born of the Spirit is spirit", as Jesus long ago made known to Nicodemus (John 3.6). And this that takes place is new birth.

What is the meaning of new birth, of being born anew (cf. John 3.3,7)? What happens when a person is born again? Nothing much happens to one's body, nor much either to one's soul, but a new birth there is indeed in one's spirit—a transformation in the human spirit takes place. That part in us that was dead because of sins and transgressions is by the Holy Spirit quickened back to life again. Yet as J. N. Darby has pointed out, it is "not only 'again', but 'entirely afresh', as from a new source of life and point of departure; . . . 'from the origin'. It is a new source and beginning of life." Hence that which was dead in us has become a new spirit, within which dwells the Holy Spirit; and so we cry out, "Abba, Father" (see Rom. 8.15,16; cf. Gal. 4.6).

❧

COMPARATIVELY SPEAKING, it may be said that the human spirit is rather young; whereas the soul in us is fairly old. And this is perhaps the reason why the soul is represented by Job and his three friends who are much older, while the freshness of the spirit is symbolized by this young man Elihu. Our new spirit is relatively younger than our soul. With this in mind, we will more likely be led to notice the humility of the spirit in Elihu. This younger man listened to the unending arguments of those older people. And yet how patiently he kept his silence.

It was the custom of the East, of course, for the young to respect the old; so that when one's elders were talking the young respectfully listened and refrained from interrupting. And this was true of Elihu, even though within his spirit he was so full that it was on the verge of exploding. Observe the very good metaphor Elihu used to describe it:

> *For I am full of words;*
> *The spirit within me constraineth me.*
> *Behold, my breast is as wine which hath no vent;*
> *Like new wine-skins it is ready to burst.* (*32.18–19*)

Yet all the while he kept his silence. Elihu was humble, courteous, patient. He waited and waited. He waited until Job's words had finally terminated. He waited until the three friends could no longer find an answer. Then, but only then, did he begin to speak. He acknowledged that the elder should speak before he did and that there should be wisdom with the aged ("I said, Days should speak, and multitude of years should teach wisdom", 32.7), and for those reasons he kept quiet throughout their long, heated, and sometimes tedious rounds of conversation.

"But," Elihu went on to say, "there is a spirit in man, and the breath of the Almighty giveth them understanding" (32.8). Thus Elihu, at the very beginning of his words, tries to convey to his hearers that he is speaking from the spirit. He is not uttering his own opinions and ideas; he is speaking as he is moved in his inner man. "True," says Elihu, "I am younger, but there is a spirit in man. It is true that you, Job, are older than I; nevertheless, we are both made by God; and furthermore, there is a spirit of understanding in man" (cf. 32.6,7; 33.6). Hence it is by the human spirit that we find that this young man at last begins to speak.

Brothers and sisters, when the soul is busily engaged, the spirit remains silent. Oh! If only, when we are plunged into a spiritual crisis, we can listen to the spirit speaking. But so very often we cannot. And the reason? Because our soul is in turmoil. How our emotion is stirring and our mind is working and our will is striving. How our whole self is caught up in a great turbulence. And when anyone is in that agitated state he cannot hear the voice of the spirit. It is too humble, it is too gentle, to interject itself into the situation. Let us realize that the inner man never forces its way. It will wait. How sensitive is our spirit.

Dear friends, I am often disturbed by one lack among believers. We do not know the delicateness of our spirit. We live such a rough and rude existence. We live such a careless life that we do not realize how sensitive is our inner man. Our spirit is like a dove. A little stirring and it is gone. It is very delicate. If we want to listen to the voice of our spirit we have to be quiet in our soul. Only after the soul has been quieted will the deepest part of our being begin to speak. And then it is that in the spirit speaking we receive interpretation.

The human spirit, as represented by the young man Elihu, is attempting to interpret Job's crisis. The soul has failed to explain or to interpret it, but now the spirit takes over and tries to do so. As the created organ for God, the human spirit—having been quickened back to life by the Holy Spirit (even as Elihu shortly declares concerning himself: "The Spirit of God hath made me, and the breath of the Almighty hath given me life", 33.4)—is in a much better position to know God and His ways. So that the words of this young man, symbolizing as they do the utterances of the spirit, are extremely important, and I would therefore hope that some time soon we all would find an opportunity to read them over very very carefully.

MOVING ON, THEN, to Chapter 33, we observe that Elihu sets forth this word to Job: "Behold, I will answer thee in this, thou art not right; for God is greater than man" (v.12 Darby). Job, you have lost sight of God. The whole trouble lies in the fact that you are intensely bound up with yourself and your own righteousness. Because of this you fail to see that God is greater than man and that it is impossible for any man to be more right or righteous than He. Your focus, therefore, is too much on yourself, whereas your sights should be set on God, and then you will see that His ways pass understanding. "Why," asks Elihu of Job, "dost thou strive against him, for that he giveth not account of any of his matters?" (v.13) Is God obligated to explain anything to you? Are you not willing, Job, to simply submit yourself to Him? Why is there not that complete abandonment to the will of God? Why do you demand an explanation as if He *must* explain? Do you not know that He is God? He is far greater than you. Can you not trust Him by faith?

Moreover, Job, is it really true that God never explains himself? That He always leaves you in the dark? Not so, not so. Though His ways are inscrutable, yet He *does* speak in order to instruct man. Said Elihu, "God speaketh . . . , though man [perceiveth] it not" (v.14). You are currently in a crisis, Job. You demand an explanation. You think God has not spoken to you—that He has not answered your prayer. But God has already spoken. Yet you have not perceived it, and that is the trouble.

It is true that in one respect God is not obligated to explain anything to us, for He is greater than man: we are simply to trust Him and yield ourselves to Him completely. In quite another respect, it is equally true that God is one who actually does speak and explain. But the fact of the matter is, we have not heard. This is where the problem lies. We blame the Lord as though he has not spoken to us; in reality, though, it is we who have not heard.

How does God speak? Elihu tells Job and us how—

In a dream, in a vision of the night,
When deep sleep falleth upon men,
In slumberings upon the bed;
Then he openeth the ears of men,
And sealeth their instruction,
That he may withdraw man from his purpose,
And hide pride from man;
That he may keep back his soul from the pit,
And his life from perishing by the sword. (33.15–18 mg.)

Thus how does God speak? He speaks deep within our spirit. The metaphor used here is—when one is in deep sleep; which is to say, that when the activity of man's soul has come to an end, then God opens (*uncovers* is the word in Hebrew in 33.16) his inner ears and instructs him of wisdom. In other words, God speaks in our spirit. And this is none other than "the anointing" spoken of elsewhere in Scripture. In 1 John 2 we read this verse: "As for you, the anointing which ye received of him abideth in you, and ye need not that any one teach you; but as his anointing teacheth you concerning all things, and is true, and is no lie, and even as it taught you, ye abide in him" (v.27). John is saying here that you do not need anyone to teach you, because there is that anointing within and it shall teach you in all things. Obey the teaching of the anointing and you shall abide in Christ.

How does God therefore speak? He speaks with a still small voice to our spirit (cf. 1 Kings 19.11–12). Our spirit is the organ for His utterance. If we are quiet enough, if all the strivings of our soul have come to rest, then we shall hear with our inner ear the utterances of God. It is the speaking of the indwelling Holy Spirit. Our human spirit is merely the organ. But the Holy Spirit is the Inhabitor. He dwells in that inner organ of ours. But very often because our soul is so agitated it cannot hear the voice of God. It is only when our soul has ceased its activity that our spirit is at last able to hear the still small voice: This is the way, walk ye in it (Is. 30.21). And as the Holy Spirit is speaking, the still small voice in our spirit will show us our pride: it will reveal our self: it will keep back our soul from going down to the pit (33.17–18). The way our soul so often is traveling is a going down to the pit. But how can we gain or keep our soul? Only by our losing it. We think we keep it by gratifying it, but the word of God declares that if anyone loses his soul for the Lord's sake he shall gain it to eternity (John 12.25).

BUT DOES GOD speak more than once? Most certainly He does. Listen to Elihu as he tells forth for God: "God speaketh once, yea twice, though man regardeth it not" (33.14). Yes indeed, God speaks once and twice. He is continually speaking; but because we do not always listen to Him, He has to speak again and again to us.

Yet this same verse 14 can be given a second rendering: "God speaketh in one way, yea, in two, though man regardeth it not." Hence God is not limited to only one way of speaking; He has another way. And what is that other way? Elihu continues to provide the answer. The second way is that

> [Man] *is also chastened with pain upon his bed,*
>   *And with continual strife in his bones;*
> *So that his life abhorreth bread,*
>   *And his soul dainty food.*
> *His flesh is consumed away, that it cannot be seen;*
>   *And his bones that were not seen stick out.*
> *Yea, his soul draweth near unto the pit,*
>   *And his life to the destroyers. (33.19–22)*

When we do not hear His first way of speaking, God has to speak in another manner. But this second time is not in the strictest sense a speaking; it in a sense is working. Hence Madame Guyon has observed that God's speaking is God's *working*. When He speaks, He works.

In what way does God work? He will raise up circumstances. He may bring in affliction, even sickness, as in the case with Job. He will so arrange our environment and bring in afflictions, sicknesses, sufferings, trials, persecutions, or whatever it may be, that through all these happenings we may see the hand of God—the chastening of the Lord. God may therefore speak to us through the illumination of the indwelling Holy Spirit or He may speak to us through the discipline of the Holy Spirit in arranging our environment. Often we are not quiet enough to hear the still small voice within us. Consequently, God has to raise up a tumultuous environment, that through all the noisy upheaval of His arranged circumstances we at last may hear His voice. If we cannot hear the whisper of the Lord, then He must thunder it. Are we so dull? Are we, like Job, so slow that we cannot even recognize His hand in our environment?

WHAT IS THE meaning of all those things which happened to Job? In a word, it is the chastening of the Lord. Job is not being punished here; it is not that he has sinned and therefore God is meting out punishment to him. No, no, no. Let us not misunderstand God by presuming that He is cruel and is punishing His servant. Not at all. Job is instead under the chastening hand of the Lord. But why? Because God deemed him to be a son of His and not a bastard. What happened to Job was not a matter of punishment; it was a matter of discipline. God disciplines those who are His own children that they may grow up into maturity. He has to train every son of His in order to perfect him. Read Chapter 12 of the Letter to the Hebrews in the New Testament and this is what you find it to be. Those whom God loves (and certainly such are His sons and not bastards) He will chasten, and scourge every son whom He receives (Heb. 12.6). It is none other than the discipline of the Lord. It is the chastening of the Lord. It is the child-training of the Lord. And this is the meaning of everything which had come upon Job.

The reason God's servant was plunged into such critical times is not because he had committed any sin, though he was not sinless, but because the Lord wants to perfect him, to mature him that he may be a partaker of the divine nature. During the period of such chastening there is grief, but afterward there will emerge the peaceful fruits of righteousness (Heb. 12.10,11).

And this is what Job's situation is all about. This is the content of God's speaking to him this second time. Although His ways and thoughts are higher than man's and beyond his understanding, God does speak once and twice in order to instruct man. The ways He speaks and unveils himself to man are therefore two-fold: once by revelation, but second, also by discipline. And all His ways are good and for the sake of saving our souls completely.

WHY IS IT, though, that Job (and we too for that matter) did not understand? Elihu supplies the answer. We need an interpreter:

> *If there be with him a messenger,*
> *An interpreter, one among a thousand,*
> *To show unto man what is right for him;*
> *Then God is gracious unto him, and saith,*

The Spirit's Interpretation

Deliver him from going down to the pit,
I have found a ransom. (33.23–24 mg.)

Job needed an interpreter, but he had none until Elihu
arrived on the scene. Yet once this young man appears
the spirit's interpretation readily comes forth to Job:
"You will not die; you will not go down to the pit!"
Dear friends, our own human spirits as enlightened by
the Holy Spirit of God will discover that discipline unto
sonship is based on the redemptive work of our Lord—
"Deliver him from going down to the pit: I have found
a ransom!" And because we are ransomed and redeemed we become the children of God. Therefore,
discipline or chastening is something having to do with
sons, not with bastards.

Who, then, is Job's interpreter? Of course Elihu is
his interpreter. He is trying to interpret to him what is
the meaning of the crucible of trials. And I believe that
in the person of this young man Elihu, Job has heard
the spirit's interpretation. And in a sense it can be said
that this was the right interpretation. Job had continually been asking, Why?, and here he finally got the
answer. The answer was not founded on the fundamental truth or principle of sowing and reaping—of God
punishing the wicked and rewarding the righteous—but
was grounded in the fact that the Lord was dealing with
Job on the basis of a higher truth: the higher principle
of discipline. He intended to bring Job into maturity,
but in order to arrive at this end he must go through a
series of trials. And this was what Elihu, Job's interpreter, gave as the explanation.

Who, though, is the interpreter today for us? None

other than our own human spirit. That innermost organ of ours is an interpreter of God. It is by this part of us within that we today interpret the workings and the speakings of the Holy Spirit. And we, like Job, may at some time in our spiritual life enter upon an experience similar to his. True, on occasion we are punished by God because we sin, and that is the principle of sowing and reaping; but at other times we know deep within our heart that so far as we know we are clear before the Lord, and yet things occur about which we do not know why. But we have a human spirit; and if we listen carefully enough to it there will come the interpretation: God is chastening His own that they may be brought into maturity.

How important it is for us to listen to the voice of the spirit. If we do not listen to that voice, if we do not hearken to our inner man, and even though God may speak and He may work, we will still not understand and we will still go down to the pit. How very important is our human spirit. It is the organ in us for God. It is not by our soul that we search Him out. It is in our spirit that we come to know Him and to know His will.

THE YOUNG MAN spoke three times. He spoke, then he stopped. He spoke again, and halted a second time. And he spoke yet once more, and stopped still a third time. Why? Because, as you will recall, there had been three rounds in the debates between Job and his friends. They had gone through one round, then another round, and a final round. And Elihu did the same thing. Voicing what is recorded in Chapters 32 and 33, he in his first speaking told Job that God is greater. He tried to interpret the way of God to him by saying that it is the disciplining and the chastening of the Lord. Do not despise His chastening nor grow faint under it, because He is treating you as His son. You should appreciate this, Job, for God is trying to deliver your soul.

Elihu, after speaking as he was moved by the Holy Spirit, finished his first utterance. And upon finishing his words, he looked around. Especially did he look at Job. He was expecting that he would most certainly respond (33.32). For Elihu had been telling him the real meaning of all his trials. Assuredly, therefore, he will be grateful and will thank him for it. But Job kept silent. He uttered not a word. Did his silence indicate he had nothing to say? Quite the contrary, it signaled Job's defiance of Elihu. He was not accepting this young man's interpretive words. He did not appreciate them. Moreover, the three friends, silent as Job was, had nothing responsive to say either. Through and through, Job's entire self was defiant.

As a consequence the anger of Elihu is stirred up. How do we know? Go through Chapters 34 and 35 and you will immediately sense that Elihu has almost become another person. Both in content and in attitude he has turned into a completely different man. He at this moment seems to have fallen into the same trap as had Job's three friends. For the argument which he now musters in these two chapters is nothing but a repetition of what they had accused Job of. Like the three friends earlier, Elihu in his second speech commences to charge Job with being a worker of iniquity: "What man is like Job, . . . who goeth in company with the workers of iniquity, and walketh with wicked men?" (34.7,8) Moreover, he echos the same sentiments that the three friends had uttered continually: "Yea, of a surety, God will not do wickedly, neither will the Almighty pervert justice" (34.12). Now how has such a reversion come about? What has happened?

Dear friends, this phenomenon discloses what the human spirit is. What in reality is a human spirit? What is its nature? A human spirit is but an organ. May I say, that a human spirit is a vacuum. It is intrinsically neutral. It can either be inhabited by the Holy Spirit and thus be under His influence, or it can be invaded by the soul and thus express the faults and failings of the self. Such is our human spirit.

PROBABLY WE DO NOT sufficiently apprehend as we ought the true nature of a human spirit. Most often we tend to think that it is all right: whatever comes from the human spirit is right and must be right. I would hasten to disagree. Call to mind that unusual occurrence recorded in the Gospel of Luke. On one occasion the Lord Jesus was traveling toward Judea and passed through Samaria. And the Samaritans would not accept him because his face was set inflexibly toward Jerusalem. They were so prejudiced against the Jews. And we will recall that the two sons of Zebedee, James and John, incensed by this reaction, came to Jesus and said, "Lord, wilt thou that we bid fire to come down from heaven, and consume them?" What did the Lord Jesus do? He turned and rebuked them, saying, "Ye know not what manner of spirit ye are of" (9.51–56 mg.).

Let us not think that because something comes out from the spirit it has to be right. Not necessarily so. When the human spirit is under the power of the Holy Spirit it speaks for God, but when it is invaded by the soul it becomes a spokesman for the self-life. And this is precisely what we have in the case of Elihu. At the beginning he spoke under the influence of the Holy Spirit and thus he spoke for God. But when he noticed that Job was defiant and that there was no verbal reaction forthcoming, Elihu's own self gained control over his spirit and he began to speak like a man not any different from the others. He had lost his spiritual sense in the face of Job's unyieldedness. With his spirit stirred to anger, Elihu forfeited any semblance of spiritual sensitivity. It was still the spirit all right, but what kind of a spirit was it? It had become a highly unsympathetic one, a spirit that now denounced Job with great vehemence. Oh how changeable is the human spirit!

Beware, dear friends. Even the innermost part of our being needs to be purified. For note what 2 Corinthians 7.1 tells us to do: "Having therefore these promises, beloved, let us cleanse ourselves from all defilement of flesh and spirit, perfecting holiness in the fear of God." Not only our flesh, but even our spirit, needs to be purified.

Thank God, though, this young man spoke the

length of these two chapters, and abruptly ceased. Did Elihu begin to realize who now was speaking? Did he sense what was happening? Most likely he did. He ceased his words. But after a slight pause he proceeded—for the third time—to open his mouth, and out came the contents of Chapters 36 and 37. Yet how opposite in tone. "Suffer me a little," resumed Elihu softly, "and I will show thee that I have yet words for God" (36.2 Darby). The spirit of humility once again came over him.

Without any difficulty you can notice whether the human spirit is under the control of the Holy Spirit or under the influence of the soul. You can easily distinguish it. The spirit which is under the power of the Holy Spirit has a distinct ring of humility about it—even the humility of the Lamb. But when it is under the influence of the soul, you quickly sense that an unseemly arrogance is present.

A SPIRIT OF humbleness descended once more upon the young man, and he said, "I will yet speak for God. I am not speaking for myself anymore. That is futile. I acknowledge my fault. I am hereafter going to speak for God again." Elihu's spirit is at this moment recovered. And he returns to the subject of discipline:

> *Behold, God is mighty, and despiseth not any:*
> *He is mighty in strength of understanding. . . .*

He withdraweth not his eyes from the righteous:
  But with kings upon the throne
He setteth them for ever, and they are exalted.
  And if they be bound in fetters,
And be taken in the cords of affliction;
  Then he showeth them their work,
And their transgressions, that they have behaved
  themselves proudly.
  He openeth also their ear to [discipline],
And commandeth that they return from iniquity.
  If they hearken and serve him,
They shall spend their days in prosperity,
  And their years in pleasures.
But if they hearken not, they shall perish by the
  sword,
  And they shall die without knowledge. (36.5,7–12)

What he this time says is a re-emphasis upon the
chastening of the Lord, but with a warning added: If
you listen and humble yourself, Job, you will enjoy that
union with God even more; but should you not hearken,
you may end up in disaster.

There is an important truth in what Elihu has just
said, and we need to pay some attention to it. Why have
we been calling Job's situation a spiritual *crisis?* Because
at the end it may turn out either way. Sometimes a
crisis will make you, but at other times it has the
possibility of breaking you. It may perfect you or it may
ruin you. It all depends on whether you and I will yield
or not. Hence Elihu's warning is an attempt to help Job
out of his soul into his spirit, for only there will he begin

to understand the working of the Lord in terms of His discipline.

❧

FROM THE DISCIPLINE of God Elihu next moves on to speak of the government of God: "Behold, God is great, and we [comprehend] him not; the number of his years is unsearchable" (36.26). There is such a thing called God's government. And we may describe it in the following manner. God is great. He governs the universe. He governs all according to His will. And if only we know His government, if only we learn to yield ourselves to His rule, we will not suffer loss. His ways are inscrutable, His thoughts much higher than ours. His government is admittedly beyond our comprehension; but if only we are willing to submit and to abandon ourselves to His authority, we shall find God's government to be most benevolent in character.

Now as Elihu was speaking to Job in this way a storm began to gather. There was lightning. There was thunder. There was darkness, wind and rain. And as the storm grew in intensity he spoke of it as a wondrous work of God which passes human understanding. The storm is part of God's government, and Elihu—wise young man that he was—used this natural event to describe that government. And in describing the aftermath of a storm, Elihu made these observations:

> *And now men cannot look on the light when it is*
> *bright in the skies,*

When the wind hath passed, and cleared them.
Out of the north cometh golden splendor:
   God hath upon him terrible majesty. (*37.21–22 mg.*)

After the storm, he explained to Job, there appears the golden light in the north. When the harsh winds have passed away and cleared the skies of every cloud and mist, there shines forth a splendor of gold so bright that men cannot look upon it. Truly, concluded Elihu, "God hath upon him terrible majesty." Do we grasp the symbolism here? Job had entered into a personal storm full of lightning and thunder, wind and darkness; but after the storm there will be that golden sunlight of unimaginable splendor rising above the horizon of Job's limited and faulty apprehension of things; and such forms a vivid picture of the government of God in its majestic yet benevolent character.

Unfortunately Job had misconstrued God's ways with him as being like poisonous arrows—"arrows of the Almighty" he had called them (6.4). But we of a later day know how unfairly he has misunderstood God; for out of the book of Jeremiah we can hear the *divine* estimate of God's ways: "I know the thoughts that I think toward you, saith Jehovah, thoughts of peace and not of evil, to give you a latter end and hope" (29.11 Darby mg.). Dear friends, this is the end of the Lord, is it not, how that He is full of tender compassion and mercy in His dealings with each one of us. Oh, the unspeakable splendor of God's ways! His government, His rule, His sovereign ordering in our lives, is indeed unto peaceful purpose and untold goodness.

❧

FINALLY, BY WAY of conclusion, Elihu in his very last words points Job to the proper apprehension of God and His rule—one of reverential fear and humility:

> *Touching the Almighty, we cannot find him out:*
> *He is excellent in power;*
> *And to justice and plenteous righteousness he*
> *doeth no violence.*
> *Men do therefore fear him:*
> *None clever in heart shall see him.*
> (*37.23–24* ASV *mg., Darby mg.*)

Surely it must be acknowledged that the voice of the human spirit under the guidance of the Holy Spirit speaks clearer than the voices of the emotion, the mind, and the will of man's soul ever can. Praise be to the Lord for an Elihu! Praise be to the Lord for the spirit's interpretation.

Our Heavenly Father, we do desire that You will bring us out of our soul and into the spirit. Yet not that spirit which is influenced by our soul, but a spirit under the control of Your Holy Spirit. Even though our emotion, our mind, our will are in utter turmoil and confusion; nevertheless, Lord, in our spirit may we see You. May we hear You. May we understand You. O Lord, teach us how to yield ourselves to Your government, knowing that the Lord is full of tender compassion and merciful. Work, Lord, and perfect Your new creation. And we shall give You all the glory. In the precious name of our Lord Jesus. Amen.

PART FOUR

God's Appearing

Who is this that darkeneth counsel without knowledge?
*   I will demand of thee, and declare thou unto me.*
Where wast thou when I laid the foundations of the earth?
*   Declare, if thou hast understanding.*

Hast thou an arm like God?
*   And canst thou thunder with a voice like him?*
Deck thyself now with excellency and dignity;
*   And array thyself with honor and majesty.*
Pour forth the overflowings of thine anger;
*   And look on every one that is proud, and bring him low.*
Then will I also confess of thee
*   That thine own right hand can save thee.*

—THE LORD GOD TO HIS SERVANT JOB

Behold, I am of small account;
*   What shall I answer thee?*

I know that thou canst do all things,
*   And that no purpose of thine can be restrained.*
Therefore have I uttered that which I understood not,
*   Things too wonderful for me, which I knew not.*
Hear, I beseech thee, and I will speak—
*   I had heard of thee by the hearing of the ear;*
But now mine eye seeth thee:
*   Wherefore I abhor myself,*
And repent in dust and ashes.

—JOB THE SERVANT OF GOD

God's Appearing

THE WAY of the Lord has now been opened. The young man Elihu had only been preparing for His advance. He had so prepared Job's heart that the latter was now ready to hear directly from God. Or to put it another way, Elihu had prepared the way of the Lord so as to enable Him to appear to Job. Up until this moment God had not been able to appear to him because of the agitation in his soul. But whenever anyone is turned away from the confusion of his self-life to a listening to the voice of his spirit, then that one is ready to hear from God. It is only in the spirit realm that spiritual problems are solved. It is only in the spirit that God can ultimately appear. Once Job had been quieted in the soul and was ready to listen to the voice of the spirit within him the way was opened for the Lord to enter the picture. And in such a state as this God finally appeared to Job in his spiritual crisis.

In this connection, we need to understand that a spiritual trial is never over by merely having an interpretation. The trial is over only when God appears to you. Very often we think if we can simply have the right explanation from God, then our problem will be solved. This is not true. God sometimes *does* condescend himself to interpret things to us, but dear friends, even with the right interpretation your crisis is not yet over. Only when the Lord appears to you can that be said. Is it not true in our spiritual life that we are all the while thinking: If only I can explain, then I am satisfied. However, we know more than we need to know already, and yet we are not satisfied. Nothing can solve our spiritual problem, nothing can lift us out of a spiritual crisis, save the appearing of God. The solution is not in searching, the solution is not in interpretation—not even in the right interpretation; the solution is solely in God himself. In God himself appearing.

Now IT WAS in a whirlwind that the Lord chose to appear to Job (38.1, 40.6). You will remember that a little while before there had been a thunderstorm, but after the storm there came forth the glorious sunshine. And that event had well symbolized the experience of Job. At this moment, though, God speaks out of a whirlwind. We know that when a whirlwind strikes it blows fiercely and sweeps away everything, destroying all in its path. It lifts up within itself everything from the earth. For a time it whirls aimlessly around and around, making for confusion and ultimately sweeping away whatever is before it.

We can say, can we not, that this too has been the experience of Job. Once again, a natural phenomenon—this time a whirlwind—is most appropriate in serving as a picture of Job's personal experience. For is he not in a whirlwind? Is he not himself being shaken and driven and whipped about? Is not everything around him being smashed and destroyed by a whirlwind-like event? Job is being turned around and around; he is losing his footing, becoming puzzled about everything; he is being uprooted from the earth, drifting uncontrollably in the air—and not knowing where he is destined to end. So that for him, all is nothing but chaos and disorder. The destructive whirlwind does indeed accurately mirror Job's situation.

More than likely, however, we would not think that God could ever be in a whirlwind. Can the Lord ever be in such confusion? How can God ever be found in such an event? Yet it is God who not only *sends* the whirlwind but who also is *in* the whirlwind, and Job shall find him there. Yet how can this ever be?

Well, we must take note of one thing good about a whirlwind. Does it not go upward to heaven? As it whirls and swirls about, it hurls into the air whatever may be in its way. It lifts out of the earth any object before it and flings it upward to heaven. Spiritually speaking, how frequently God has to use a whirlwind to deliver us out of ourselves into God himself! It is a terrible experience, yes; but thank God, He appears right there in the whirlwind and speaks out of the whirlwind. Very often, in our time of prosperity and tranquillity, we do not hear His voice. But in the most unlikely situation—in a whirlwind even—we find not only the voice of God but also the presence of God. It is an experience not very different from that of Moses when confronted in the wilderness by the burning bush wherein the Lord's voice and very presence were made known. Yet by such an experience a person shall be brought nearer to the Lord.

Recall that day when Elijah was ready to leave this earth and go to God. Elisha his disciple followed him over the river Jordan. And we will remember that, as they were talking, a chariot of fire and fiery horses separated Elijah from Elisha. Now some people believe that the Lord's prophet rode on the chariot of fire into heaven. But if we read the Bible carefully we will know that this was just not so. The chariot of fire and the horsemen did in truth divide Elijah from Elisha; but it was a *whirlwind* which took the elder prophet up. Elijah was raptured in the whirlwind. (See 2 Kings 2, esp. vv.1 and 11) And this is similarly what we see in the case of Job. This poor man is going to be delivered completely out of his self. There on the dung heap he has been sitting, all bound up with himself: so full of self-love, self-pity, self-righteousness, self-vindication. And the Lord has been whirling him around and around, but will finally one day very soon rapture him out of himself into God.

UNFORTUNATELY, Job's three friends had been quite wrong about God, for they had held such a transcendent view of Him that they thought He would never condescend himself to speak and to argue with men. To them He was too great and too high to be bothered with such business. He had consequently become for them a God who hides himself, a distant and impersonal deity. Now such a view is admittedly majestic and noble, but it lacks the intimate and personal touch. In their opinion, God is most surely transcendent but He is far from being immanent.

Job's conception of God was much better than that of his friends. He realized that the Lord is not a distant monarch, but that He is willing to condescend to man; He will not terrify man with His strength and power. Job clearly knew God better.

Yet Job can be faulted too. His error lay in thinking that he could reason with God as though God could be wrong. He had continually tried to argue what he did not understand. For at the very beginning of God's speaking out of the whirlwind, the Lord asked this: "Who is this that darkeneth counsel by words without knowledge?" (38.2) He was referring here not to the three friends but especially to Job, for the latter subsequently acknowledged that this was so when he later echoed these very words of God and applied them to himself: "Who is this that hideth counsel without knowledge? Therefore have I uttered that which I understood not, things too wonderful for me, which I knew not" (42.3).

God has His counsel which is beyond our human understanding, but we often obscure His counsel, as did Job, by trying to argue or to explain it. Unconsciously, Job had overstepped the proper bounds in his familiarity with God. Familiarity is good; but as the saying goes, it sometimes breeds contempt. And to the three friends, Job had appeared as one who was not only wicked, but *arrogantly* so. Yet God understood His servant and answered his prayer by appearing to him and speaking with him; nevertheless, at the same time He had to correct his wrong attitude. We must not overlook the fact that the Lord's way with Job—in His appearing and in His speaking—was not only sympathetic (we must thank God for that), *it was also strict.*

AND SO OUT OF the whirlwind God began to speak to Job (38.1ff.). Very strange to say, though, He did not explain. Do you find anywhere throughout the response of the Lord to Job any explanation for what had happened to him? None at all. Job had said to the Lord (cf. 31.35), Here am I: this is my situation: now therefore answer me: will you please explain it? Dear friends, as we approach the Lord how often our mentality, like Job's, is full of petitions for an answer: Answer me! Give me an explanation and I am satisfied. Then everything, we believe, will be all right. Yet if we know God we realize this is not the right approach to such a situation. The Lord does not owe you or me an answer. He is God. He is greater than man. There is no need for Him to explain His action. Job demanded an answer from God but what did God do? Instead of answering him, He put to His insistent inquirer even more questions than Job himself had asked. God's response was an avalanche of His own questions.

I cannot tell you how many questions you will find

as you read Chapters 38 and 39. I tried to calculate how many God actually put to Job, yet each time I counted I came out with a different number. So I do not know for sure. I only know that the total exceeds 50. Job had petitioned the Lord with but one basic question, yet He turned around and asked him more than 50 of His own! Here might we learn a lesson: that it is not for us to ask God questions, it is for Him to do the asking.

Let us inquire, though, why the Lord should put all these questions to Job. These two chapters in which they are recorded are actually some of the most beautiful and sublime portions of Scripture. In them God asked His servant question after question concerning His creation: "Where wast thou?" "Hast thou?" "Knowest thou?" "Canst thou?" "Dost thou?" "Wilt thou?" etc., etc. God spoke of His creation of the earth, the sea, and the cloud, the morning, the light, and the rain. He spoke of the stars in the heaven and the animals on earth. Lo, when I created the earth where were you, Job? When I laid the foundation of the earth did you do anything? When I fixed the sea in its boundaries did you help Me? When I apportioned morning to the day that everything might be enlightened, what had you done, Job? When I entered into the depths of the sea or fathomed the gates of death, did you know anything about such matters? Who brought about the rain? Who is the father of the dew drops? Did you bring forth the stars in the heavens? Consider all the animals—the ostrich, the horse, the eagle, the ass, the goat—they are all different. Now who supplies them with good? Do you, Job? Who gives them intelligence? Who leads them? Can you tell Me anything about this?

✤

AND ON AND ON AND ON, over 50 such inquiries. Yet all these were put forth with but one purpose in mind. It is found in the words of Chapter 40. The Lord inquired: "Shall he that will contend with the Almighty instruct him? he that reproveth God, let him answer it." And Job replied, "Behold, I am nought: what shall I answer thee?" (vv.2–4a Darby) In a sense Job had been contending with the Almighty; it appeared as though he would instruct God; he seemed to be reproving the Lord for what He had done to him. By all those 50 queries and more God had ultimately come down to this one question for Job: Shall the one who contends with God Almighty instruct and reprove Him?—Then let him answer. In effect the Lord was chiding His servant: "You want to instruct Me? All right, go ahead! You want to reprove Me? Very well, proceed to correct Me!"

How subtly and foolishly we may allow ourselves, as Job did, to fall into such a false position. We would never deliberately take such a wrong attitude, yet easily will we be tempted into it. We would never consciously and purposely assume that we know more than God or that we can instruct Him or that we can even reprove or correct Him. We would never dare do this, because we know that He is greater than any man or all men put together. Without realizing it, however, as we become wrapped up in ourselves, we can drift into a kind of mental stance whereby we begin to assume we know more than God and that He has got to explain His action.

In other words, how easy it is for us to forget ourselves—yet not in the right but in the wrong sense of forgetting who we are and what we are. The direction of our forgetfulness is totally wrong, for because we love and pity ourselves so much and try to justify ourselves so greatly, we unconsciously forget who and what we *really* are. We inflate our own self-estimate to such a degree that we begin to consider ourselves equal with God, and sometimes even superior to Him. We need to be reminded again and again that He is the Almighty— that He has the right to do anything He likes—that He always knows what He is doing. The One who creates all and governs all cannot be ignorant of what He is undertaking. And He knows best, because He *is* the Almighty.

Dear people, let me say again that it is not an explanation we need. Job had received that already through Elihu, hence God did not explain anything. No, not an explanation but a right attitude of heart is what we need. God has to cut us down to size. He has to bring us to our senses. He has to drive us to that position where we see we are nothing. Especially does He have to do this with a man like Job, who was perfect and upright, who feared God and abstained from evil, and had flourished under the gracious hand and blessing of the Lord. Whoever has a great deal is tempted to feel that he has now become somebody, that he has a right to make demands. But at least one thing is sure to happen if God should ever appear to us without explaining himself: He will bring us to our senses by trimming us down to the right size, wherein we begin to see, and to confess along with Job: "I am nought, I am nothing: what shall I answer You, O God?"

In some translations of this passage in 40.4 (the Authorized Version, for example) it even is rendered, "I am vile"!—Not only am I nothing, but even I am *terrible*. How dare I speak without knowledge! Only an appearing of God will ever make us truly see ourselves. The Lord hammered away at Job with question after question, declaration upon declaration, until at last he saw himself as he really was: that in comparison to God he was of little account, that in fact he was nothing.

In Job's case, of course, all God's questions and declarations were related to creation, because it was the Old Testament period. In our day, however, whenever the Lord shall appear to us, there will not only be statements and interrogations relating to creation, there will also be those connected with redemption: "I have done this to redeem you, I have performed that to set you free. Was I not crucified for you? Have I not shed My blood for you? I have given My life for you. But what have you done in this regard? Have you done anything? What is it that you possess that was not at first given to you? What that you have is really yours? Am I not the Lord? And do you not therefore owe everything to Me? And do I not have a right over you? Can I not do whatever pleases Me? Is there not a reason for My working? Why can you not trust Me? Why must you question Me? Can you not abandon yourself to Me?

Do you not know that I am God? I am your God, but what are you? Nothing! Nothing at all!"

⚜

IF THERE HAD not been in Job's experience an appearing of God such as this, then all his trials would have ended up in vanity. Would have been to no positive purpose. Why, in the final analysis, does this good man suffer? For no other reason than that he may be brought to his own end, that he may at last bow down and say, I am nothing. Oh how difficult for the Lord to bring any of us to a death position, especially when we are blessed by God, especially when we have achieved something. But oh how easy for us to become proud and to think that we now know something, we now have a right. We easily forget that we are but a cipher: that before the Almighty we *are* nothing: that before the Almighty we *know* nothing. It is very hard for us to see ourselves as He sees us.

We therefore need the crucible of trials in which to be ground into such nothingness; and this most blessed position is something which God has to bring us into, otherwise we cannot be fully united with Him in one spirit. We have to be reduced to zero in order to make real in our lives the truth of what Paul said: "He that is joined unto the Lord is one spirit" (1 Cor. 6.17). It is not a matter of the satisfaction of the emotion, nor of the understanding of the mind, nor of the gratification of the will; it is a union of spirit. But when our soul is so big, we are not able to be united with God in one spirit.

Only a seeing of ourselves as we truly are can ever bring us into closer union with God. But how do we see ourselves? Solely by first seeing Him. So far as experience is concerned the whole trouble with our union with the Lord is not because He is great. It is because we are *too* great. It is not the *smallness* of man which hinders this union, it is his *greatness*. Unless we are brought to nought, such a union in spirit with God is most difficult. Our self has to be crushed, to be smashed, to be broken. Only then can our spirit be one with the Lord's. His Spirit has then become our spirit: we humbly realize we are nothing, only containers for His occupation.

Consider the earthly life of our Lord Jesus. He who is equal with God, and yet He emptied himself. He took upon himself the form of a man. He took the position of a slave. He humbled himself, becoming obedient to God even to the point of death, and that the death of the cross (see Phil. 2). He became nothing but a container for God's occupation. Said He repeatedly: I can *do* nothing: I can *speak* nothing: I *am* nothing: I am only doing what the Father does and saying what the Father says. As Son, Jesus learned obedience through sufferings (Heb. 5.8). As Son, He is chastened of the Father, that is, He is child-trained by the Father. This is one of the greatest lessons to be learned, that one is nothing. And because the Lord Jesus became *nothing*, therefore God for Him was *everything*.

How often we say, God is everything. But is He in fact everything? Let me tell you, if we are not being brought to nothing, how can He possibly be everything? We are simply too big. It takes a crucible, a grinding, a deeper working of the cross, many sufferings perhaps, to bring us to that place of nothingness wherein we confess, I am nought—I am vile. Whenever God appears to you and me this will inevitably be the result. Call to mind the experience of Isaiah. What happened when God appeared to him in the temple? What was the reaction of the prophet when he saw the Lord in His glory? He cried out and exclaimed: Unclean! I am unclean! I am a man with unclean lips dwelling among a people of unclean lips. Woe to me! Or call to mind the experience of Daniel, who when he saw the Lord fell down as one dead. Said he, All my comeliness has turned into corruption (see Is. 6; Dan. 10). When the Lord appears, man simply crumbles.

Do you say you have seen God? Do you say you have met God? What really do you mean? Very often you actually mean you have received some light from Him: you are being enlightened: you know something about Him: you can explain: and you can now instruct people. Or, what may often be meant is that you have even arrived somewhere morally, spiritually. Is this not in fact what you mean? Well then, if that is the case, you have not seen God. Yes, you have heard Him. But you know Him only by hearing, not by seeing Him. For if you truly see Him the one unmistakable mark in your life will be, "I am nothing; I am nought; what ever can I say to You, God? Yes, I have much to say, but I can no longer utter it."

YOU KNOW, the sign of a child is talkativeness. A child

speaks a great deal. He is a constant chatterer. But the sign of a mature person is silence. He knows too well to be talkative. His response is, "What can I say before God? There is nothing any longer to be said." Like Job, who is now being brought to maturity, he will more than likely say:

> *What shall I answer thee?*
> *I lay my hand upon my mouth.*
> *Once have I spoken, and I will not answer;*
> *Yea, twice, but I will proceed no further.* (*40.4b,5*)

It was the overwhelming sense of his own nothingness before God which shut Job's mouth. Not because he had no more to say, but what *can* he say since he is nothing. Here is a deeper lesson for all of us to learn. We may have lots to say, yet what can we utter once we realize who we clearly are? By this we have taken a great step forward toward maturity.

How our experience coincides with Job's. Whenever we achieve (so we think) a little bit of spiritual advance, we tend to be self-righteous and become self-confident. We now believe we know better; we are even tempted to question God at times. We become bold in ourselves and not necessarily in Christ. We forget our real position and condition. We have a great deal to say. And why? Because we are still children. But as the hand of the Lord comes upon us, we are gradually brought to see how we are nothing, and what can we then say? Like Job, a silence comes over us which is the mark of maturity.

❧

BUT DO YOU THINK this is all God said to His servant? Not so. He spoke to him in *two* parts. The work upon Job begun in the first part of the Lord's appearing (told in 38.1–40.5) was not yet finished. Much still remained to be done. And hence in the second part (40.6–42.6) we see that God had to speak again, and in His speaking the second time we find He raised even additional questions. Still responding out of the whirlwind, He asks Job: "Wilt thou even annul my judgment? Wilt thou condemn me, that thou mayest be justified?" (40.8) As if to say again, Does not God know what He is doing? Is there not a reason for it? Why can Job not trust in God and allow Him to finish His work?

Interestingly, we find by this time that the parties involved have become simply God and His servant. Satan does not come into the picture at all. The Lord does not reveal in the slightest to Job that what has involved him in such a trying way is the great conflict raging in the unseen realm. The negative has altogether been left behind. What is currently uppermost is the positive working of God to perfect His servant, to make him a mature son. For the Lord at this time shifts to the moral side of things. In particular, He asks Job whether he is able to bring the proud down:

> *Deck thyself now with excellency and dignity;*
> *And array thyself with honor and majesty.*
> *Pour forth the overflowings of thine anger;*
> *And look upon everyone that is proud, and abase him.*

Look on every one that is proud, and bring him low;
*   And tread down the wicked where they stand.*
Hide them in the dust together;
*   Bind their faces in the hidden place.*
Then will I also confess of thee
*   That thine own right hand can save thee.* (*40.10–14*)

It is the moral glory of the Almighty to bring the proud down: "God resisteth the proud," says the apostle, "but giveth grace to the humble" (1 Peter 5.5b). But does Job understand that such is God's moral glory, and even if he does, is he able to effect such a work as this? Are you able, asks the Lord, to humble the pride—even your own pride, Job? For what hinders him from entering into the full maturity of sonship is his pride. He has been greatly blessed by the Lord, and he has progressed well beyond his contemporaries. But without realizing it he has become proud of himself, forgetting that it has been all of God's grace. And hence the Lord is compelled to use two creatures from the animal world as object lessons to drive home to Job this serious matter of pride. God vividly paints before him a picture of both the behemoth and the leviathan.

WE DO NOT KNOW for certain what two animals these terms refer to. Most likely the behemoth is the hippopotamus and the leviathan has reference to the crocodile. And in describing these two beasts at some length,

God calls the hippopotamus "the chief of my ways" and labels the crocodile "the king of all proud beasts" (40.19 and 41.34 Darby). These animals are fierce, uncontrollable, proud, fearing nothing. None else in the animal kingdom can subdue these two proud creatures, but can God? But then too, who can subdue the proud Job? Certainly none else in the kingdom of men, but can God? In citing these beasts the Lord was in effect saying to Job: "I created this hippopotamus and this crocodile along with you [see 40.15]. Like the hippo, you are as a king among men. Like the crocodile, you are a proud and uncontrollable creature. *But,* are you beyond Me? You are beyond the control of others as are the hippopotamus and the crocodile, but are you beyond My control? Am I not able to do something to you? Am I not able to rein you in?"

I hope each time we go to the zoo and observe a hippo that we see ourselves; that every time we behold a crocodile we see our own persons. For this is what we are: haughty and lordly beasts! How proud, brothers and sisters, we all can become. And this was what Job had become. And if you care to call pride a sin, then that was Job's sin. Job is righteous, yes; but he became so *self*-righteous that he sinned against God in being proud (cf. 32.1,2b).

Hence the Lord is as much as saying here that: "The reason why I deal with you is to humble the pride. You are too proud, Job. You are too proud of yourself and of your spiritual achievement. I therefore took all your virtues and all your works away so as to lay you bare to see whether you could still be proud. I have dealt with you in this manner in order to take away your pride so that you might submit yourself with humility into My hands for the maturing and perfecting work which is yet to be done."

Is IT NOT A paradox that, to grow from a child to a son, we have to return to being childlike in confidence and in faith? Unless we be converted and become like a little child, said Jesus, we cannot enter the kingdom of God (Matt. 18.3). As Psalm 131 makes so plain, we must be weaned, like a child upon the mother's breast, if we are to hope and to trust in the Lord (vv.2–3). The more one is like Christ the more childlike (though not childish) he becomes; for notice how the Lord Jesus lived on the earth. How much like a child He was: neither speaking, nor teaching, nor doing, nor going anywhere even—but what first He heard or saw His Father so speaking or doing. Let us see that it is not in the *complexity of life* that maturity is reached, but rather, spiritually speaking, it is in the *simplicity of Christ* that sonship is gained. Pride is the full expression of self, and therefore thwarts the maturing process; whereas humility is self-less, and therefore manifests God.

Now AFTER THE Lord had so spoken and so revealed

himself to Job, he yielded with humility and confessed to God in the following manner:

> *I know that thou canst do all things,*
>   *And that no purpose of thine can be restrained.*
> *Who is this that hideth counsel without knowledge?*
>   *Therefore have I uttered that which I understood not,*
> *Things too wonderful for me, which I knew not. . . .*
>   *I had heard of thee by the hearing of the ear;*
> *But now mine eye seeth thee:*
>   *Wherefore I abhor myself,*
> *And repent in dust and ashes.* (*42.2–6*)

He finally gives the Lord His rightful place. O God, confessed Job, You *are* great; You can do anything, it is within Your right; and if You have a purpose, no one can hinder it, for Your thought is best. O God, Your purpose is not one of harshness or of cruelty, but it is good—yet I did not know it. Wherefore I abhor myself, and I repent in dust and ashes.

Job abhorred himself. From this we can discern that he was being brought into even a *lower* position than nothing. Previously he had been brought into nothingness: "So far as I am concerned," he had earlier acknowledged, "I am nought, I am nothing." But here he has become *less* than nothing. Says Job: "I loathe myself; I am afraid of myself. How terrible I have been. How could I have raised myself up against God? How could I have ever questioned Him? I uttered what I did not understand, things that were too wonderful for me which I did not know anything about. Oh! Why should

I have questioned Him? Does He not indeed know what He is doing? I should trust the Lord. I should abandon myself to Him. Why should I any longer hold on to myself, to this nothing? Nay, to this self that is worse than nothing? I abhor myself, and repent in dust and ashes."

Dust and ashes. Job had mentioned this once before. Read Chapter 30 and you will discover that in the midst of bewailing his wretchedness he had said that God "hath cast me into the mire, and I am become like dust and ashes" (v.19). Yet had he really? Had Job at that time actually accepted such an estimate of himself? Continue to read the rest of his words until they are eventually terminated at the conclusion of Chapter 31 and you will learn that he had not really considered himself to be dust and ashes. For there we witness how he protested far too much concerning his own righteousness and integrity of life. Dust and ashes? I am afraid not. In effect Job had said, "I am not dust and ashes; I am a precious stone."

Quite frankly, when we sometimes say "O Lord, I am but dust and ashes", others will know by the very tone of it that what we really mean is: "I am a precious stone." You and I do not mean the other at all—We do not want to be dust and ashes. For to be *that* is to be nothing. And who wants to be nothing? But in Chapter 42 we find that Job has been brought to the place where he has gladly become dust and ashes: Yes, God, You have reduced me to ashes, to the very last form there can be; but I gladly accept it. I know myself, and I now know You also; for my God, I have *seen* You.

❧

Do LET US REALIZE, dear friends, that there is a great difference between knowing God by hearing and knowing Him by seeing. Job confessed that his knowledge of God in the past had come by hearing; which is to say, that it had been indirect and informational in character and had therefore not been intimate, personal, and experiential enough. It had been more a mental than a spiritual knowledge. Such a knowledge is entirely inadequate, since it puffs up a person instead of bringing him low. Knowing God only by hearing makes one into a somebody, but knowing Him by seeing reduces one to a nobody; to dust and ashes. And this was truly Job's experience. Through the Lord's painful dealing, he has at last seen God. Through the Lord's affliction he has come into a very close and personal encounter with Him.

It is good that in afflictions we meet God. It is He who solves our problems, yet not by explanation but by appearance. Our problems are solved when we see Him. For when we see God, we are not so much concerned with our problems as we are concerned with *ourselves* being the problem; so that we abhor our very selves and repent in dust and ashes. In giving up ourselves we receive more of God, just as John the Baptist expressed it when he confided, I must decrease but He must increase (John 3.30). As we become nothing, God becomes everything.

How then do I know that I have seen God? I know whenever I become dust and ashes: whenever I abandon myself to Him since now I am less than nothing and He has become everything to me: He is God: He is all. And when that point is reached, *the crisis is over.*

THE WORDS OF Scripture tell us that the Lord "blessed the latter end of Job more than his beginning" (42.12). What *was* the latter end of this man? The reader of JOB will see that the prose part of his story is resumed at Chapter 42.7 and concludes the entire book a few verses later. And in this closing segment we are told what his latter end was.

First of all, "the captivity of Job" was wonderfully "turned" by the Lord (42.10). We do not know how long a time had elapsed between the first part of his story (Chapters 1–2) and this latter part which is before us here. His captivity may have lasted for several months or for several years. No one can be certain. But what we do know is that after God had spoken to him and he had learned his lesson, Job's awful captivity came to an end. We can now recognize that God's chastisement has been for good purpose. It has been educational, and will always be terminated when the aim has been achieved.

In this regard, we need to take to heart the words of admonition given by the psalmist David: "Be ye not as the horse, or as the mule, which have no understanding; whose trappings must be bit and bridle to hold them in, else they will not come near unto thee" (32.9). Let us not give resistance to God's dealings, but quickly draw near to Him in ready submission because His chastisement is unto positive purpose.

IT IS INSTRUCTIVE to note, however, that Job's captivity comes to a close only when he prays for his three friends (see 42.10). We must notice that just before this God had spoken to Eliphaz, severely reprimanding him and his companions: "My wrath is kindled against thee, and against thy two friends; for ye have not spoken of me the thing that is right, as my servant Job hath" (42.7). They had spoken from their soul, but Job had spoken from his heart. Their words may have appeared to be more logical and authoritative, yet such utterances were not at all spiritual. On the other hand, Job's words may have sounded unreasonable and even rebellious; nevertheless, they were real and sincere. Their souls, therefore, needed to be atoned for and purified. Hence a burnt-offering was called for by God as the means of His acceptance of them. Said the Lord to Eliphaz and his friends:

> *Take unto you seven bullocks and seven rams, and go to my servant Job, and offer up for yourselves a burnt-offering; and my servant Job shall pray for you; for him will I accept, that I deal not with you after your folly; for ye have not spoken of me the thing that is right, as my servant Job hath. So Eliphaz . . . and Bildad . . . and Zophar . . . went, and*

did according as Jehovah commanded them: and Jehovah accepted Job. (42.8–9)

From all this, we see that Job's soul had at last been brought to rest. All the activities of his soul, as represented by the three friends, had been quieted. He had been able to listen to the spirit's interpretation and had ultimately been brought face to face with the Lord. Reduced to ashes and dust, Job now experienced God as having become all things to him. Here is a man who is therefore presently living in God in the spirit; and because of this, all the various parts of his soul (as symbolized by Eliphaz, Bildad, and Zophar) are now to be redeemed, atoned for, purified, and brought under the control of his own spirit. So that we see that much earlier there had been first the *dividing* of the soul and the spirit in Job (cf. Heb. 4.12), but that there is currently to be a bringing of the soul into *subjection* to the spirit. And this is the significance of the burnt-offering for Eliphaz and his companions. Such an offering was the salvation, as it were, of Job's soul. The soul must submit to the spirit, no longer trying to dominate over the heart. Job is at this moment living in the spirit and thus has his soul delivered because he is now accepted before God.

WE HAVE MENTIONED the turning of Job's captivity as being one very important feature in the latter end of

Job. But what further can be said about his latter end? Well secondly, it constituted the end or purpose of the Lord concerning Job's life. As we said at the very beginning of our study, God's end in view is sonship as the right of the firstborn. Dearly beloved, who is really the firstborn? Is he not our Lord Jesus Christ, who is the only begotten Son of God? So far as His eternal relationship with God the Father is concerned Christ is the only Son: there is no other (cf. John 1.18, 3.16,18; 1 John 4.9). But so far as His relationship with the creation, and especially the church, is concerned, Christ is the firstborn Son.

This can be seen clearly when we consider the following passages from the Scriptures:

When he bringeth in the firstborn into the inhabited earth he saith, And let all the angels of God worship him (Heb. 1.6 mg.). Who is the image of the invisible God, the firstborn of all creation (Col. 1.15). And he is the head of the body, the church: who is the beginning, the firstborn from [among] the dead (Col. 1.18a). For whom he foreknew, he also foreordained to be conformed to the image of his Son, that he might be the firstborn among many brethren (Rom. 8.29). For it became him, . . . in bringing many sons unto glory, to make the author of their salvation perfect through sufferings. . . . He is not ashamed to call them brethren, saying, I will declare thy name unto my brethren. (Heb. 2.10–12a)

In other words, the only begotten Son of God the Father came into the habitable world with a very definite purpose in view of bringing many other sons to glory;

and because of that, the Lord Jesus is called the Firstborn. God is out to secure for himself many other sons after the order of His firstborn Son. As the Firstborn, the Lord Jesus is the Son of the strength of the Father. He is therefore the exact image of the Father (Heb. 1.3). And those whom God has foreknown He has also predestined to be conformed to the image of His Son so that Christ should indeed be the firstborn Son among many brethren who have taken their very character from Him.

Hence what is the eternal purpose of God? It is that through our Lord Jesus Christ, the Firstborn, we may all be brought to glory as sons of God by our having taken up His Son's character because we have been conformed to His image. Christ has been so wrought into us by the work of the Holy Spirit that we take on His personality and character—Christ is formed completely in us, even as Paul expressed it (Gal. 4.19). What God's firstborn Son is, so we his many sons are to be.

With the result that not only has Christ become the firstborn among His many brethren but also He has transformed us into the "church of the firstborn" (Heb. 12.23). In relation to all creation, we who comprise the church have become the church of the firstborn. Because the Head of the church is the Firstborn, therefore we who are His body, the church, are also the firstborn. In other words, in Christ we are made heirs of God and co-heirs with Christ (Rom. 8.17). We are to receive from God as His heirs that which is the right and blessing of the firstborn. What a precious salvation this is. This is the *real* end and purpose of the Lord: that we may be made the sons of God and so share the right of the Firstborn of God. And this is the whole lesson of the book of Job.

YET HOW DO WE know that in his latter end Job was promoted to the right of the firstborn? What indication do we have that the end and purpose of the Lord—sonship—was finally achieved in his life? We have three evidences given to us in the narrative's final segment, Chapter 42.7-17.

First of all, in verse 10 there is the matter of the double portion: "And Jehovah gave Job twice as much as he had before." God blessed Job doubly in granting him a double portion of everything he had hitherto possessed and lost. We must look more closely into this to see exactly what is meant by the term double portion. Perhaps a few references from the Scriptures may be helpful in our understanding it. We should first read Deuteronomy 21.16-17 where we learn that a double portion is the birthright of a firstborn son: "In the day that [a man] causeth his sons to inherit that which he hath, . . . he shall acknowledge the firstborn . . . by giving him a double portion of all that he hath; for he is the beginning of his strength; the right of the firstborn is his." Here we learn that because the firstborn is the son of a man's vigor and strength, he receives a double portion of his father's wealth and substance as the right of the firstborn.

There are other Bible references to double portion as

well. Recall the prayer of Elisha: "Let a double portion of thy spirit be upon me" (2 Kings 2.9). The words of Paul also: "Let the elders that rule well be counted worthy of double honor, especially those who labor in the word and in teaching" (1 Tim. 5.17). Moreover, in Jesus' parable of the talents, note how the five earns five more and the two earns two more (Matt. 25.14–30). All these instances in Scripture are additional examples of the idea of double portion.

But the life of Job is likewise an instance of one who receives a double blessing. His wealth, all which he had possessed formerly, was increased to him twice as much: whereas previously Job had had 7,000 sheep, he now had 14,000; whereas before he had possessed 3,000 camels, currently he had 6,000; whereas earlier there had only been 500 yoke of oxen, he could at this moment number 1,000; and whereas before he numbered only 500 she-asses among his possessions, today he could count 1,000 of them (cf. 1.3 with 42.12). How God blessed His servant indeed!

Surely it can be said that the Lord's end for Job had been reached, that from being merely a child and an adolescent he has grown into mature sonship wherein he receives a double portion of God's blessing as the right of a firstborn son. But this is God's purpose in Christ Jesus concerning all of God's own, even the church of the firstborn. All those who through suffering arrive at sonship shall have a double dispensing of God's blessing. As heirs of God and joint-heirs with Christ, they too may receive the double portion—they shall inherit the unsearchable riches of Christ (Eph. 3.8,18).

❧

But a second evidence that the Lord's goal of sonship for Job had been achieved is shown in the matter of priestly function and its enlargement. This was referred to briefly in discussing the turning of Job's captivity, but it needs to be enlarged upon here in relation to a somewhat different subject. In 42.8 we saw how God demanded that Eliphaz and the other two friends take bullocks and rams to Job. But Job not only offers up to God these burnt-offerings for his friends; he also, at the behest of God, offers up prayers for them. Says God to Eliphaz: "My servant Job shall pray for you; for him will I accept, that I deal not with you after your folly" (42.8b). We see that God accepts Job and forgives his friends.

Now is not this that Job has done verily the work of a priest? At the beginning he only offered burnt-offerings for his family, but today he offers on behalf of his friends. His priestly function has thereby been enlarged. And is this not the case with all who have learned under the governing hand of God? As they are maturing into sonship they shall be able to help many people in their spiritual needs. Then prayers shall be heard and offerings shall be accepted. Many shall be brought into an acceptance by God through their ministry.

❧

And the final evidence of sonship in Job is that there is for him a large measure of spiritual increase. This is indicated by what we find in 42.13–17:

> *He had also seven sons and three daughters. And he called the name of the first, Jemimah; and the name of the second, Keziah; and the name of the third, Keren-happuch. And in all the land were no women found so fair as the daughters of Job. . . . And after this Job lived a hundred and forty years, and saw his sons, and his sons' sons, even four generations. So Job died, being old and full of days.*

God, we see, had now given His servant seven new sons and three new daughters. We must recognize the fact that the sons and daughters whom he had had before were, yes, born by the blessing of God, yet they were *naturally* possible since he was at that period a young man. But at this time he was probably 70 or even 100 years old. Humanly speaking, therefore, Job was not able to father sons and daughters anymore; nevertheless, we now find a spiritual increase of such purity that there were depths to it. Imagine, *seven new sons!*

Offspring in the Scriptures, as we noted already, have spiritual significance. Sons, we know, represent strength; daughters, on the other hand, symbolize virtues. Unlike the sons, the daughters' names are specifically mentioned in this passage to show how definite and substantial are these virtues of Job. The names given to the three daughters are very lovely. Jemimah, the first daughter's name, means "beautiful as the day"—that is, a vibrant and living beauty, a moral character as bright as daylight. Actually, there are two kinds of beauty. One kind is like an artificial flower. There is no question that a false flower does possess a beauty, yet it is a dead and lifeless sort. But there is another type of beauty which is vibrant and full of life. And this is the kind which Job's first daughter represents. So that we may say that henceforth the virtues of Job are all as beautiful as the day. They are like the day: full of life and therefore fruitful, full of the fruits of the spirit.

The second daughter's name was Keziah. Keziah means "cassia", a flower which is extremely fragrant and used for making perfume. Job's virtues are full of fragrance, even the fragrance of Christ. And the third daughter's name, Keren-happuch, signifies "horn of paint". Horn stands for power: the power of God, the authority of Christ. In sum, then, here is to be found such spiritual increase in Job that it is full of beauty, full of fragrance, and full of power and authority.

But Job had seven new sons as well. And he was not only able to see his own sons, he was able to see his sons' sons also, even as far as to the fourth generation! How very productive, how extremely fruitful Job now is in the spirit. How large is the measure of his spiritual increase, both in terms of character and spiritual strength.

SUCH IS THE Lord's latter end in Job's life. The Lord's purpose has finally been reached. And, as the apostle James has so succinctly put it, we have heard of the endurance of Job but have also seen the end of the Lord, *how that He is full of tender compassion and pity.* Was not this true with Job in his day, and is this not still true with us in our own day? Oh the splendor of His ways with us! God has no desire to make His own to suffer. He allows sufferings solely to bring in maturity, He permits trials solely to perfect in us His glorious purpose. His is indeed a kindly and compassionate way with us, if only we can perceive it as such and gladly accept it as such. Hence, may the end and purpose of the Lord be achieved in each of our lives. And then the story of Job will be our story too.

Our Heavenly Father, we have learned of the endurance of Job and have also seen the end of the Lord. We agree and gladly affirm that the Lord is full of tender compassion and merciful. How we praise and thank You, because Your thoughts concerning Your people are noble and manifold. How we praise and thank You that You are not content with our remaining as little children, but Your desire is that we should grow into sonship so that we may be heirs of God and co-heirs with Christ. Oh what a blessing! Lord, do open our eyes and our understanding that we may see the goal which You are after, and that we may endure the cross because of the joy which is set before us. May we look up and away to Jesus, the Author and Perfecter of our faith. We bless You. We praise You. In the Name of our Lord Jesus. Amen.

A Note on the Author

Stephen Kaung was for many years a fellow-worker of Watchman Nee in the work of the Lord in their native land of China. In 1949 the author left his homeland and ministered for several years in other areas of the Far East. In 1952 and for nearly two decades afterward Mr. Kaung lived in New York, where he labored faithfully among the Lord's people. Since 1971 he and his wife have made their home in Washington, D.C., where he continues to serve the Lord in various avenues of ministry.

Mr. Kaung's service to the saints of God in the area of Christian literature has in recent years been the translation into English of a number of Mr. Nee's works originally published in Chinese. Mr. Nee, who died in 1972 after twenty years' confinement in a Communist prison for the sake of his faith, is today acknowledged as having been one of the outstanding Christian leaders of this century in China. *Ye Search the Scriptures* and *The Basic Lesson Series* (to be 6 vols. when completely published) are but the latest of his works to be translated by Mr. Kaung.

The Splendor of His Ways is the second of Mr. Kaung's own books, his first having been published in 1970 under the title of *The Songs of Degrees, Meditations on Fifteen Psalms*. Both are published by Christian Fellowship Publishers.